CW00616591

Thinking Things

General Editors
Graham Slater and C. S. Rodd

2. Worship

Thinking Things Through

Already Published

The Bible
C. S. Rodd

In Preparation

The Christian and People of Other Faiths
Peter D. Bishop

Why Evil and Suffering?
C. S. Rodd

The Sacraments
Michael J. Townsend

Is There Life After Death?
C. S. Rodd

Thinking Things Through

2. Worship

Michael J. Townsend

EPWORTH PRESS

ISBN 0-7162-0513-0

First published 1997
by Epworth Press
20 Ivatt Way,
Peterborough
PE3 7PG

Typeset by C. S. Rodd
Printed and bound by
Biddles Ltd
Guildford and King's Lynn

Contents

General Introduction

The great German theologian, Hans Küng, has said that his aim in all his writings is to enable his readers to hold their faith with confidence and not with a bad conscience. This new series, prompted by the conviction that Christians need to think through their faith but often lack appropriate help in so doing, has a similar aim. Moreover, the assistance that it seeks to offer is related to another conviction: that many church members need persuading that theologians are concerned in any way with their problems and that theology can be at all relevant to their lives.

In such a situation, it is essential, we are sure, to begin with life and with church life. Only in that way can we be confident that we are dealing with grassroots issues. Plainly, however, it is not enough to identify the questions where they arise; we must also indicate the sources of help – if not of all the answers – in as non-technical a way a possible.

In some volumes, these tasks will be tackled in sequence; in others, they will be interwoven. Whatever the precise format, however, our hope is that, through this interaction, difficulties will be faced, fears dispelled, open discussion promoted, and faith informed and strengthened.

The books can either be read by individuals on their own or used in groups. We hope the questions at the end of each chapter will be useful both as a check that the text has been understood and as a spur to reflection and discussion.

Later volumes will deal with such issues as the Christian and people of other faiths, the problem of evil and suffering, the sacraments, life after death, Jesus, the Holy Spirit, creation, salvation and discipleship, prayer, making moral decisions, science and religion, and presenting the gospel.

GRAHAM SLATER AND C. S. RODD

Introduction

This book is rather different in layout from its predecessor in the series. A brief opening chapter is designed to raise some of the general issues about worship. The five remaining chapters each begin with a housegroup discussion, followed by a section headed Reflections. The Reflections are sub-divided into numbered sections. At the end of each numbered section there are questions for discussion.

If this book is used for group study, it may be helpful to begin by reading the housegroup discussion at the beginning of the chapter concerned, and then deal with as many of the numbered sub-sections as the group wishes. The questions which have been provided are only suggestions, and groups may find that different ones come readily to mind.

I hope that readers will find the housegroup discussions credible and realistic, but it needs to be pointed out that neither the housegroup members themselves, nor any of the characters to whom they refer in the course of the discussions are based on actual people, living or departed.

When writing about worship it is often helpful to give specific examples. I have usually drawn these from my own Methodist tradition, but hope that readers from other traditions will be able to adapt what is here without any difficulty. In a short book on a major subject, much must necessarily remain unsaid and it has not always been possible to indicate alternative approaches. Those wanting a more comprehensive treatment will find many books available to meet their needs and some of these are mentioned in the list of books for further reading.

For readers in many Christian traditions, however, it will seem very strange that even a short book on worship does not deal with the sacraments, and in particular, with Holy

Communion. This is quite deliberate because a separate volume on the sacraments is planned for later in the series.

This little book is dedicated to the Ministers and Local Preachers of the Leeds Methodist District, my colleagues in leading worship week by week.

Michael J. Townsend
October 1996

1

Raising Some of the Issues

Julie, normally a bright and bubbly person, was in a thoughtful mood when she joined the other members of the housegroup for their regular Tuesday evening meeting. John, quiet and reserved himself, was usually good at spotting changes of mood in others. 'Come on, Julie,' he said, 'there's something on your mind. Do you want to share it with us?' Julie took a deep breath and began.

'It's something my friend Fiona said at work today. We were having lunch together in the canteen and I mentioned that I had a busy week ahead at church. Fiona said, "It's strange really, I don't miss it at all." So I said, "What do you mean? What don't you miss?" And she said, "Church." I never knew she went to church. Well, she doesn't, that's the point. But it seems that she used to; regular as clockwork, every Sunday up until about three years ago, she said. Then, one Sunday morning, in the middle of a long reading from Revelation she thought to herself, "What am I doing here?" She'd never thought anything like that before and it made her a bit scared. She said her father had been a clergyman and church had always been part of her life. Then suddenly, just like that, she couldn't see the point of singing hymns and listening to sermons. So she stopped going.'

After a moment Christine remarked, 'You do sometimes hear about people who lose their faith suddenly.' 'Oh no,' Julie said, 'she hasn't lost her faith. That's what I assumed, but she told me she still believes in God and says her prayers when she feels she needs to. She decided that Sunday worship was just a meaningless habit she had fallen into and that you can be a perfectly good Christian without going to church.' Christine looked across at Julie. 'And you are wondering what you can do to help her find her way back to worship?' There was a pause and then Julie slowly nodded her head. 'Well, yes I suppose so, but there's a bit more to it than that.' The other members of the group made encouraging noises so, after another pause, Julie continued. 'Actually, I'm wondering whether Fiona might not be right. As you know, I grew up in the church just as she did. I came through Sunday School, Brownies, Guides, Youth Club and into church membership, and church has always been part of my life too. I've never really thought about why I go on a Sunday and I'm wondering whether it isn't just a habit with me, just like it was with Fiona.'

Alan, Christine's husband, said quickly, 'There are good habits as well as bad ones, Julie! I suppose you could say that going to church is a habit with me. It has been for nearly seventy years. But it's a good habit to get into.' Julie looked unconvinced. 'But is it?' she said. 'What does it do for me? What did it do for Fiona if she doesn't miss it now? And I've been thinking about Mike.' Several heads nodded sagely. The housegroup had heard about Julie's husband from time to time; a cheerful happy-go-lucky agnostic, who would do anything for anyone – except come to a church service. 'You see,' Julie continued, 'Mike is a very happy and contented person yet he never seems to feel the need to come to worship, and there are lots of other people like him. So what I am wondering is: why *do* we worship, and what does it achieve?'

Mollie was the first to respond. 'I would have felt like that a few years ago, but that was before I met Jesus. After Sean and I split up, but before the divorce, I went to church a few times with a friend from work. I couldn't see the point of it all; it was like an alien world. When I became a Christian it all seemed quite different. Of course, I had a lot of learning to do. I didn't know the hymns or anything and I couldn't find my way round the pew Bibles at first, but that didn't seem to matter very much. I just wanted to be there and to praise God for giving me a wonderful Saviour in Jesus. You see, Julie, when your faith is really alive you just want to worship God – that's all there is to

2

it.' Tom then chipped in: 'Not quite, Mollie. It isn't as simple as that. Sometimes it is worship which keeps you going even though it can be very hard to take part in it. When our teenage son Paul died in that motorbike accident more than fifteen years ago, going to church was very difficult for me and Betty. We didn't feel much like praising God for anything. We were really kept in the church because we felt it was a praying community which surrounded us with love when we most needed it.' Betty nodded her agreement and added, 'There are still some hymns I can't bring myself to sing, but worship gave us both something very important, and still does. I agree with Alan really. If it's a habit, it's a good one! You can come to church for years without thinking about it but then, when you really need an inner strength, there it is, though I can't quite explain how.'

'But wouldn't that still be true,' asked Christine, 'even if you never came to church but just stayed at home and read your Bible and said your prayers? Wouldn't you be just as much in touch with God that way? Why do we need to come together in church for that?' 'Well,' said Marian thoughtfully, 'there's the sermon of course. We have to be in church in order to hear it and we often get some help from it.' This was Alan's cue for a favourite grumble. 'Not as often as we should,' he said. 'When I was laid up with my leg in plaster a few years ago, I listened to the service on the radio most Sundays. I heard some very good sermons; proper sermons, like we used to get in church.' Tom broke in before Alan could get into his stride. 'Yes, but what you miss when you stay at home and watch the service on the television or listen to it on the radio is *other people*. What matters is the friendship you find when you come to church.'

'You're all missing the point!' said Mollie, heatedly. 'You don't need church to find friendship and support. People find that in many different organizations, such as the Women's Institute or a Rotary Club. What is distinctive about the church is that we come together to worship God!' 'Yes Mollie,' said

Julie quietly, 'we know that. You've only brought us back to the beginning of our discussion! What we don't seem to have sorted out is why we need to worship, and what worship is all about.'

The members of the group fell silent. They were quite used to discussions which went round in circles; that didn't really matter very much. It was more important that everyone had their say and shared their experiences. In the process, usually anyway, they learned something from each other by the end of the evening. But on this occasion Julie was making a valid point. It did seem a bit odd that after half an hour's discussion they appeared to be no nearer answering Julie's question, or to meeting her personal need, than they had been at the start. Yet each of the group members was a regular attender at church services.

John hesitated before he said, 'We've all said quite a bit about what we *get* from going to worship. For Betty and Tom it is a sense of a loving community which prays and cares. For Alan it is a sense of stability in a changing world. For Marian it is the opportunity to hear a good sermon which offers help in living the Christian life day by day. For you, Mollie, though you may not quite realize it, it is the opportunity to find emotional release through praise.' Mollie started to say something, but changed her mind. John continued: 'None of those things are wrong in themselves, but what is odd is that none of us, myself included, has said much about what we *give* in worship. Perhaps, in a way, we started with the wrong question. After all, Julie's friend Fiona was really saying, if I understood correctly, that she had stopped getting anything out of going to worship. Isn't that right, Julie?' 'Yes,' said Julie, 'I think that's fair comment. But it isn't really a wrong question to ask is it?' 'Well, perhaps not a wrong question to ask, but I think it might be the wrong place to begin,' John replied. 'Mollie, I hope I didn't sound rude just now; I didn't mean to be. I don't easily use the kind of language which comes

4

naturally to you, but I think I know what you mean. When you spoke about wanting to praise God I felt we were beginning to get close to the heart of the matter.'

This was the longest speech anyone had ever heard from John and no one was quite sure what to say next. It was Christine who noticed that it was nine o'clock, time for coffee and biscuits!

2

An Act of Worship

Members of the housegroup were quite excited. Their discussion about the nature of worship had caught their interest so much that some of them were still talking about it the following Sunday morning, after service. When he heard about this Stephen, their minister, had an idea. 'We often learn more about something by doing it than by talking about it,' he said to Mollie. 'How about the housegroup leading the evening service in a few weeks' time, when I am planned to preach? I'd better do the sermon, if you decide to have one, because none of the group is an accredited preacher. But you plan the worship, and I will fit in with what you want.'

Mollie consulted the others and they agreed to have a try at what Stephen had suggested. Stephen was not able to be present at their next meeting, but he had promised to be with them the week after, though only if they decided a sermon ought to be included!

When the housegroup came together on Tuesday evening, Alan handed out pieces of blank paper and pens. Then he said, 'I'm not quite sure where we start. Do we begin by choosing the hymns, or the theme of the service, or what?' 'I think we ought to have hymns that everybody knows,' said Betty. 'It does make such a difference to the singing and we only have a small congregation in the evening.' There were nods of agreement at this, but before they could pursue that topic, Christine said, 'Well, I think we ought to decide right at the start to include the young people. After all, we are always saying at Church Council that we ought to get them more involved in things.'

'But Christine,' said Tom, 'the young people don't come to the evening service. We are a small congregation and mostly over forty.' 'I know we are usually,' said Christine, 'but the youngsters might come if we asked them specially, and I'm

sure they'd be pleased if we gave them something to do.'
'Sorry, Christine,' answered Julie, who was a Junior Church
teacher. 'It just doesn't work that way. I know our young
people, and they would find that very patronizing. In any case,
it's no good just giving them something to do. We need to find
out what they are good at and what they want to do if we expect
them to be involved.' There was a pause whilst the members
thought about that, and then Marian said, 'Yes, it wouldn't be
very practical, Christine. In any case, I'm not sure that it would
be right. Surely we need to think of the people who are usually
there, and plan worship which they will appreciate. After all,
it's their service really, isn't it?'

Alan spoke up: 'We've been talking for fifteen minutes, and I
haven't written anything down yet.' 'I know how you feel,'
said Betty soothingly, 'but we did need to decide whether or
not to accept Christine's suggestion. Perhaps you're right,
though. Let's make a start, shall we?' For a few moments the
group members looked at their blank papers. Then Marian said
brightly, 'Well, let's begin with a hymn, like we usually do.'
'Don't we usually begin with the notices, so as to get them out
of the way?' asked Alan. 'You're forgetting that since Stephen
came we've been having the notices duplicated. We don't read
them at all now,' said Christine. 'Of course, how silly of me,'
Alan responded. 'And since we don't have a choir in the
evening any more there isn't an introit either. Marian's right,
let's begin with a hymn.' And very firmly, Alan wrote
'HYMN' on his paper.

'I don't see why we have to begin with a hymn just because
we always do,' said Mollie. 'Sometimes at the morning service
we have a few songs and choruses before we start – you know,
pre-service worship. It would make a nice change to do that in
the evening as well.' 'That's something which has always
puzzled me,' said John. 'How can there be such a thing as "pre-
service worship"? I mean, surely we are either worshipping or
we are not! And, in any case, what's the point of it?' 'The point

of it,' Mollie replied, 'is that it sort of warms us up before the service itself – not before we start exactly; I realize that if we are singing we have already started, but before we begin the – ' she paused. 'What was that word the preacher used about the service the other week?' 'Liturgy,' said John. 'Liturgy!' exclaimed Julie. 'I hope we aren't going to have any liturgy in our service! I don't want something read out of a book, I want something spontaneous.' 'Well, it won't exactly be spontaneous, will it, not seeing as we're supposed to be planning it tonight,' said Tom. 'And, in any case, I expect we shall be reading out of one book – the Bible – *and* singing out of another one.' Hastily, Marian said, 'I think that's quite a good idea of Mollie's. We could begin with a few songs that everybody knows to get us in the mood.' Alan sighed, and added 'OR SONGS' to what he had already written.

'That's decided, then,' said Mollie brightly. 'Which hymns or songs shall we have to start?' 'I know that "The day thou gavest Lord is ended" is a great favourite of Mrs Kemp, and she's always at evening service,' said Betty. Julie protested: 'Oh Betty, we can't just have hymns because they're somebody's favourite, otherwise we'd sing the same hymns every week! In any case, "The day thou gavest Lord is ended" is a hymn for the end of the service, not the beginning.' There was a slightly awkward silence before Mollie said, 'I think we had better leave the choice of hymns or songs until later. What we really ought to be doing now is to decide on the theme of the service.' 'Does a service always have to have a theme?' asked Marian. 'Some of them don't seem to.' 'It's always better when they do,' said Christine. 'In any case, it makes our job much easier. Once we have decided on a theme we can find four or five hymns and a couple of Bible readings on that theme without too much difficulty.'

'There's something not quite right about that,' said Tom. 'I have a feeling it ought to be the other way round.' 'What, you mean you choose the hymns and readings first, and then choose the theme?' asked Christine. 'Perhaps not the hymns,' Tom replied. 'I think it might be best if we chose the Bible readings first and they would, as it were, settle the theme of the service for us. Then we choose the hymns to fit the theme. What I'm not quite sure about is how we choose the Bible readings.'

Alan spoke up again. 'We've now been talking for three-quarters of an hour, and all I've written down is 'HYMN OR SONGS' so we don't seem to be getting anywhere.' 'Don't be so irritable dear,' said Christine. 'It isn't very easy planning a service and we have to be patient with each other. I think Tom's right, we need to choose the Bible lessons. Let's have the one about John the Baptist preaching in the wilderness.' Tom protested: 'I hope this doesn't sound silly, but I think it's the wrong time of the year for John the Baptist. We usually read about him on one of the Sundays before Christmas, and this service we're planning will be in the middle of July.' 'That doesn't matter, surely? We can read whatever bit of the Bible we choose!' exclaimed Mollie. 'Yes, of course we can,' replied Tom. 'I just think it would feel odd to read about John the Baptist announcing the coming of Jesus, in the middle of July!' 'Tom's right,' said Marian. 'We had a talk once at the Bright Hour, from Sandra, when she was our minister. She told us all about the different seasons of the Christian Year. There's Easter and Lent and Advent and Christmas, and some others, I think. I remember she showed us those coloured stoles she wore at communion services and told us how each colour represented a different season. Ever so interesting it was.'

'I've just remembered,' said John, suddenly. 'The Bible lessons for each Sunday are printed in the circuit plan! We should have looked at those first and then we wouldn't have wasted so much time.' 'I don't think they are,' said Christine. 'I think those are for the morning, and we are leading the evening service, so that doesn't help.' Tom fished a slightly crumpled circuit plan out of his jacket pocket and had a look. 'I'm afraid that's right,' he said. I'm sure there used to be two lots of readings for every Sunday, but there's only one now.'

Some of the initial excitement had now begun to wear off and the housegroup was beginning to be just a touch dejected. They didn't need Alan to remind them that they had been discussing things for well over an hour and hadn't actually reached any conclusions. 'Shall we have our coffee early?' suggested Betty, 'give ourselves a break, and then see if we have any fresh ideas in the last half an hour?' So they did.

When they resumed, Tom was the first to speak. 'I think we may have been looking at this entirely the wrong way round,' he said. 'We have been trying to fill in the details, like hymns and readings, before we have the shape of the service in front of us. I think we ought to work out *why* we have certain things in our worship at all, and that will help us discover how they all fit together and what order they should be in.'

Half an hour was not very long, but once the members of the group had got the idea, contributions came thick and fast. 'If the reason for reading the Bible is because it offers us insights into God's truth which we need to hear, and if we have a sermon because it attempts to unpack those truths for us today, then,' said Julie a little breathlessly, 'the readings and the sermon need to be together somewhere.' 'Yes, and if we put them together they will give us the opportunity to listen to what God is saying to us,' said John. 'What comes afterwards should give us the opportunity to make some kind of response to what we have heard.' 'We certainly can't begin by reading the Bible,' said Betty. 'I wouldn't feel ready for that.' 'Nor would I,' Christine chipped in. 'We need something at the start which brings us together and helps us to offer ourselves to God in worship before we get to the biblical readings.' 'Well,' said Mollie, 'I'm all for beginning with praise and adoration. I think we got that right, at least, in our earlier discussion.' 'You mean, when we decided to start with a hymn?' said Marian. 'Or songs,' added Mollie quickly. 'So there we have it: praising,

11

listening, responding. Is that right?' Tom asked. And yes, by and large, they all thought it was.

'We still haven't actually chosen any hymns, or readings for that matter,' said Alan. 'Not to worry; we have another evening next week to do that, and Stephen will be with us then, so we can ask his advice,' observed Betty cheerfully. 'So we are definitely having a sermon, are we?' asked Alan. They all agreed that they were. John volunteered to let Stephen know that the group wanted him to come, but added, 'Don't rely too much on being able to ask his advice. He said something to me about only contributing if he absolutely had to.' 'Well, he may have to, if tonight was anything to go by,' was Alan's final comment.

Reflections

1. *Coming Together for Worship*

One of Christine's comments about the service was, 'We need something at the start which brings us together.' We do not normally pay much attention to this, but it is quite important.

It is instructive to watch what happens in most churches in the few minutes before an act of worship begins. Members of the congregation arrive at the church building with many different things on their minds. There may be elderly people, perhaps those who have physically struggled to get to the church. There may be young parents who have worked hard to get themselves and the children there on time. They may be very aware that one of the children still has untied shoelaces, or that the money for the collection is still on the table in the hall. There may be lonely people who have seen nobody else since the previous Sunday and who arrive half an hour before the worship begins in order to chat with their friends. There may be people who need to talk with others about something which is happening during the coming week. They will be dashing around trying to make sure they don't miss anybody. There may be people coming in from the Sunday School building or ancillary rooms, having just set out the material for the Junior Church lesson.

What is really happening, is that God's people are coming from their busy everyday lives, to become a 'congregation', a community of faith meeting with God. Discipleship has been lived out and worked out, in home, office, school, factory and so on, during the week. Individual Christian people have been praising God in their daily living. There will, no doubt, have been successes and failures in that Christian living. And many of the people who come together will bring joys or fears to offer to God in the worship. As the congregation assembles, all these things are brought together.

The very act of coming together as a congregation has significance. It speaks of the way in which God calls people into community and links our individual Christian lives together so that we become a fellowship of praise and love, centred on the gospel. The manner in which worship begins needs to reflect this. When a service begins with: 'Good morning, everyone. We are sorry the heating didn't come on early enough and the church is a bit cold. Now shall we sing hymn number forty-eight?' any sense that God's people are gathering together to meet with him has gone by the opening hymn. Sometimes worship begins with the notices. The motivation is often to prevent them interrupting the flow of the worship later on, which is good. But might not notices at the beginning focus our attention on the wrong things?

Churches with choirs often begin with an Introit. In recent years some churches without choirs have the Introit sung by the congregation. This is a good way to begin especially if it is chosen so as to lead us into worship properly. Some helpful examples are: 'Jesus, stand among us' (*Hymns and Psalms* 530)

13

and 'Father, we love You' (*Mission Praise* 46). A 'Call to Worship' is also a good way to begin, and is perhaps best if it is biblical. The Psalms are a fruitful source of such material:

'Praise the Lord!
How good it is to sing praises to our God;
for he is gracious, and a song of praise is fitting'
(Psalm 147.1).

Sometimes it is sufficient for the worship leader simply to say, 'Let us worship God.'

A mood of praise and adoration needs to be established right at the start of worship. Mollie's idea of beginning with a few songs and choruses is a perfectly good one. But it is not helpful if these are regarded as a 'warm-up' session, or described as 'pre-service worship'. Wasn't John's comment about that right? Once the songs and choruses have begun, the congregation is worshipping. If the singing begins before the official service time, those who arrive at the last minute might feel that they have missed some of the worship. If there is to be more than one opening hymn or song of praise, why should this not be within the service itself?

Some churches have a problem with the congregation talking loudly, right up to the opening words of the service, and sometimes even during them! Many solutions have been tried, and none are perfect. One way of dealing with it is for someone else to announce that the worship has now begun, and the first two minutes will be spent in silent prayer. At the end of that time the worship leader enters and announces the first item. The silent prayer enables the worshippers to bring the busyness of their lives before God and to pray about the worship itself. This is quite effective in turning a collection of individuals into a worshipping congregation and, of course, there are other ways too.

FOR DISCUSSION: How does worship usually begin in your church services? Would you welcome more opportunity for quiet and prayer and, if so, how might this be achieved?

2. *Praising*

The housegroup settled on 'Praising, Listening and Responding' to describe the framework or structure of the service they were to lead. This is not the only possible structure, but it is a good one for a Protestant preaching service. There are, of course, other headings which might be used.

After the opening act of praise there is often a more reflective note in the worship. Sometimes, at this point, there will be a prayer of Adoration. Adoration is extremely difficult to define, and even more difficult to achieve! It differs from Thanksgiving. Thanksgiving is centred on what God has done for us; Adoration is about offering God worship just because he is God. 'Holy, holy, holy, Lord God Almighty' (*Hymns and Psalms* 7) is a good example of Adoration, as are 'How shall I sing that majesty' (*Hymns and Psalms* 8), and 'Ye holy angels bright' (*Hymns and Psalms* 20). Some very simple contemporary songs also manage this extremely well. Examples of these are: 'Father, we adore you' (*Mission Praise* 44) and 'Holy, holy, holy is the Lord' (*Mission Praise* 74). Such hymns and songs of Adoration are often drawn directly from biblical passages, especially Isaiah's vision in the temple (Isaiah 6), the Psalms and some passages in the book of Revelation which describe the worship of heaven.

Also drawn from the story of Isaiah's vision in the temple, is the custom of following praise and adoration with a time of Confession. It is when we have sung of the majesty and holiness of God that we become most aware of our own failures in Christian living. Spoken prayers of Confession are generally fairly short and not too specific. Many of them are constructed

15

round the commandments of Jesus, to love the Lord our God and to love our neighbours as ourselves. Brief silences, allowing time for personal recollection, can be helpful here. But we must never be left to wallow in our sins! The heart of Christian faith is not that we are sinful, it is that God is gracious. So Confession must always be followed by Absolution. In some Christian traditions only those who have been ordained as presbyters (ministers) may give an absolution. That is not the case within the Protestant churches. Those who have been authorized to lead worship, whether or not they are ordained, can declare God's forgiveness. After all, *they* are not doing the forgiving; they are declaring that God forgives, which is just another form of preaching the Gospel! So it is perfectly proper for the worship leader to say (for example), 'Hear then the word of grace: Your sins are forgiven.'

Being forgiven leads equally naturally into further praise, often with a note of thanksgiving:

> Ransomed, healed, restored, forgiven,
> Who like thee his praise should sing?

as the hymn writer puts it. So more songs and hymns of praise may well be appropriate at this point, or perhaps a canticle or psalm – read or sung.

FOR DISCUSSION: Is it always right to begin with an act of praise, or are there times when worship needs to start in some other way? If so, what might these be?

3. *Listening*

'The readings and the sermon need to be together somewhere,' Julie said in the discussion. That was perhaps the single most important insight the group reached. Methodist and Free

Church worship took a long time to realize this (though in Methodism's case there are historic reasons relating to the origins of what we call the 'Preaching Service'). At one time the readings and the sermon could be separated by almost half an hour of other items, as though they had nothing to do with one another. Keeping them together at the heart of the worship stresses that Christian preaching must always arise from God's word to us in the scriptures (whether or not a 'text' is used in the sermon). This should remind us of two things. Firstly, that the scriptures are not bits of long-ago literature which can be read and then dropped, but are vital for our discipleship today. Secondly, that a sermon must not be a preacher riding a hobby-horse, but must rather be a genuine seeking of God's word for the contemporary situation.

It is customary to have two or three readings from the Bible. These are usually (i) from the Old Testament (the Hebrew scriptures), (ii) from the Epistles (which for this purpose includes Acts and Revelation!) and (iii) from the Gospels. A Psalm may appropriately be said or sung between the first and second, and a hymn may be sung before the Gospel. In many churches there is a growing tendency to read only two lessons. When this happens, it is usually the Old Testament reading which is ignored. This is perhaps because it is often thought to be difficult or less obviously relevant to a Christian congregation. This is unfortunate, not only because much of the Old Testament is rewarding in its own right, but also because without some knowledge of it we cannot understand much of what is written in the New Testament.

FOR DISCUSSION: Does your church have pew Bibles, in which the congregation can follow the readings? If there are, has this been found helpful? If there are not, is it worth considering?

4. *Responding*

If, in our worship, we have been engaging with God and listening for God's word for us today, then there needs to be opportunity for us to respond to what we have discovered and heard. If our hearts and minds are open to God we cannot be unaffected by what has happened in the worship itself. Our lives are changed in subtle but important ways because we have met with God as a worshipping people. Hopefully, our response will not end with the close of the service, but will go on during the coming week as we seek to live our lives to God's glory. We *begin* that response within the worship itself. There is a variety of ways in which we make that response. For example, we may be moved to penitence by what we have heard, in which case the time of confession can be moved to this part of the worship. More usually, we find four main elements in our worship at this point: Thanksgiving, Intercession, Offering and Dismissal.

If the Notices are to be read, they too form part of our response to God because they are about the life of the congregation in the coming week. It will often be possible and appropriate to include some of the items from the Notices in prayers of Thanksgiving (such as thanking God for the money raised at the previous week's Gift Day) or Intercession (such as praying for the forthcoming Church Council).

a. *Thanksgiving* is more specific than Praise, because it is about giving God thanks for particular and specific things. Readings and a sermon about God's presence driving away our fears, for example, might be followed by a hymn of Thanksgiving which strikes this note (such as 'Light of the world, thy beams I bless', *Hymns and Psalms* 681). Or prayers of Thanksgiving for God's daily presence with us as individuals and a Christian community might be fitting. Other examples will come readily to mind.

b. *Intercession* is usually expressed through prayer. There are some hymns and songs which are appropriate here: *Hymns and Psalms* 412 or 413 might well be sung after a sermon on peace, for example. Intercessory prayers are one of the important ways in which the church engages with the world in which God has set it. They are intended to express our commitment to the values of God's kingdom being seen in daily life. Experience suggests that such prayers need a careful framework if they are not to become long and tedious. They may take the form of direct petition to God: 'We pray for . . .' or biddings to the congregation: 'I ask your prayers for . . .' They may include brief periods of silence, each bidding or petition concluding with a call and response. The best-known of these is:

Leader:	Lord in your mercy
Congregation:	Hear our prayer

but is that in danger of becoming stale through over-use? Any service book will offer alternatives, such as:

Leader:	The Lord hears our prayer
Congregation:	Thanks be to God

or

Leader:	Your kingdom come
Congregation:	Your will be done.

There are a number of possible frameworks for prayers of Intercession. A good example is:

i. *The world-wide church, its life, work and witness.* We pray first for ourselves, that we may be agents of God's love in the world.

19

ii. *The world and its needs*. We pray about events and situations which are causing concern.

iii. *The community around us*. We pray for the particular needs of our local situation and those who work in or serve our community.

iv. *Those in special need*. We pray for the sick, the bereaved and others in trouble. It is important not to be too specific and to safeguard people's privacy. Many churches have a book in which people can write requests for prayer.

v. *The departed*. Some Christians have difficulties with actually praying *for* those who have died. So we often use a phrase such as, 'We remember with gratitude . . . ' Names of those who have died recently can be included. Such prayers link us with the whole community of faith and the life of heaven, to which all our praying looks forward.

The Lord's Prayer is often now placed after the Intercessions rather than earlier in the worship. This is because it sums up all that we have prayed about.

c. *Offering* is not just about the money! All of our life needs to be offered in service to God and others. The collection is an appropriate focus for such a prayer. We offer ourselves and our material gifts in response to God's gracious love for us. It is a great pity when the collection is taken and dedicated earlier in the worship, perhaps before the children leave. Such a practice obscures an important part of our engagement with God.

d. *Dismissal* is far more than simply saying 'That's it; off you go!' We go from our collective worship to be the people of God in the world. We go out strengthened by our worship and fellowship, changed people. The Dismissal usually includes a Blessing. As with the Absolution, the worship leader declares God's blessing to the congregation, although some people seem to be happier saying 'us' rather than 'you'. However it is done, the Dismissal is intended to assure us of God's blessing and presence in the week ahead.

FOR DISCUSSION: Is there any difference between your own private prayers of Intercession, and those which we can appropriately offer in public worship? If so, what are those differences, and what do you find it helpful to pray about in a church service?

3

Putting Worship Together

At the housegroup's next meeting they were joined by their minister, Stephen. He was to preach the sermon at the service they were planning. Following the previous week's meeting Alan had been busy on his word-processor. When they began, he gave each member a sheet of paper on which was printed:

Praising

Hymn or Songs
Prayer (Adoration? Confession and Absolution?)
Hymn or Psalm or Canticle

Listening

Old Testament Reading
New Testament Reading
Hymn
Gospel Reading
Sermon (Stephen!)

Responding

Hymn
Any additional Notices
Prayers (Thanksgiving? Intercession?)
The Lord's Prayer
Offering and Dedication
Hymn
Dismissal

'That's the framework I think we agreed on last time,' said Alan. 'Are you happy with that, Stephen?' 'Yes, fine,' said

Stephen. 'But that isn't the important thing. As I said when I suggested you should plan the service, it's *your* service, so what matters is whether you are happy with it.'

'We've talked a bit about that,' said Marian. 'I'm not sure it is really our service either! I think the worship belongs to everybody who comes. Each of them should be able to put something in and get something out. That way we can all respond to God's love for us.' 'I agree with that,' said Tom. 'It's just that we are responsible for planning and organizing it on this one occasion. Stephen often has that responsibility, and so do the other people who lead our worship. But we are really doing it on everyone's behalf. I find that quite a responsibility - but very exciting.'

'I like what we've done so far,' said Mollie. 'And I think the structure Alan has put down is right. But it looks a bit ordinary. If we've got the chance to plan the worship, don't you think we should try and do something different?' 'Not just for the sake of being different, no I don't,' Alan responded. 'It may look fairly ordinary, but it isn't boring,' said Betty. 'At least, now I have thought about why we do things and how they all fit in, I don't find it boring. But I wonder what some of the people who haven't shared in our discussions will think about it.' 'I expect they'll enjoy it if we choose hymns they like,' said Christine. 'Which reminds me, we'd better get cracking! We've got ever so much to do, including choosing the hymns and the readings. And we haven't got a theme for the service yet. We got rather bogged down on some of those things last week.'

'Surely, the theme for the service will come out of the readings,' said Tom. 'If we find some readings on which Stephen is happy to preach, then they will suggest a theme to us.' 'Yes, but we discovered last week that choosing the readings is very difficult,' said John. 'We thought we'd solved it because the lessons for the day were printed on the circuit plan, but when we looked there were only lessons for the morning. It's the evening service we are taking.' 'Why don't we use the same ones?' asked Julie. 'After all, they are presumably the lessons for the whole day, not just for the morning service.' 'That wouldn't be very helpful to those who come to worship in the morning as well,' said Betty. 'Joyce and Jim White always come twice, so do Andrew and Pat Robinson, and Mrs Kemp and Susan Turner and, oh, there are several more who do. They wouldn't want to hear the same readings twice in one day, would they?' 'We could contact the morning preacher to see if he or she intends using those lessons. If not, we could use them,' said Tom, consulting his circuit plan. 'Oh, it's you, Stephen!' 'Yes,' said Stephen. 'I'm preaching twice that day.' 'So if we use the set readings in the evening, you would have to find some different ones for the morning,' said John. 'It is hardly fair of us to ask you to do something we are finding difficult ourselves!'

There was a pause. All the housegroup members were thinking the same thing and wondering who was going to be the first to say it. Julie took the plunge. 'Stephen, we know you don't want to say more than necessary, but we really do need your help on this one. Choosing the lessons is ever so hard. You're the one who's been trained to do these things and none of us is a preacher. Will you give us some guidance?' Stephen smiled. 'Yes, of course I will. But don't think of me as the expert. Many worship leaders use the appointed lessons most or all of the time, though some never use them at all. I expect I shall use them on the Sunday morning because I usually do. So we do need to look for something different. What we must not do, is to decide what I am going to preach about and then hunt through the Bible for some lessons which fit that theme.' 'Why not,' asked Mollie. 'I think I know why not,' said Tom. 'If we decide the theme first we are sort of telling God what we want him to say to us.' 'Oh, yes,' said Mollie. 'I hadn't thought of it quite like that.'

'Sometimes,' Stephen continued, 'I find that a Bible passage I have been using for my daily quiet time will speak to me, and then I use that for the evening service. But that hasn't happened this week. One possibility is to look at the lessons for two years' time.' 'I don't understand what you mean,' said Alan. 'Well,' replied Stephen, the lessons for the day come from a cycle of readings called a Lectionary. The one we happen to use takes four years to complete its cycle. At the moment we are in what is called Year B, the second year of the cycle. If we use the readings for the same Sunday in Year D, it will be two years since the congregation last heard them, and two years before they will hear them again!' There was a short pause whilst people worked that out. Then Betty said, 'It certainly prevents us hearing the same lesson read on three successive Sundays, as happened fairly recently. Let's give it a try.'

'How do we find out which readings they are in Year D?' asked John. 'I thought we might need a copy of the lectionary, so I brought one along,' Stephen replied, reaching into his briefcase for it. 'Tom, you've got the circuit plan, which Sunday is it when this service is taking place?' Tom consulted his plan. 'The 9th Sunday after Pentecost,' he said. Stephen looked at the Lectionary. 'The lessons for the 9th Sunday after Pentecost in Year D are: 1 Kings 17.8–16, Romans 14.10–23 and John 6.22–27.' He repeated the lessons slowly whilst everyone wrote them down. 'Let's spend some time reading them through,' said Alan. 'I hope everybody remembered to bring Bibles.' Everybody had, and the group sat in silence for a while, reading intently.

'Do you think you would be happy to preach on those?' Marian asked Stephen after a while. 'Yes,' said Stephen thoughtfully. 'On the Old Testament reading I think. It's a lovely story about how God provides for the needy through the hands of his servants. There you are: that's the theme of the sermon and that's the last word I shall say tonight – except to ask for a second cup of coffee when the time comes!'

Christine spoke up: 'At first, when I read the lessons through, I couldn't see any connection between them,' she said. 'But

26

I'm beginning to. The Kings passage is about God providing food for the widow, and the Gospel is about working for the eternal food that Jesus gives (though I think I need that explaining properly to me). Romans is a bit more difficult. It seems to be about not giving offence through the food you eat. I'm not sure where that fits in with the others. Still, I'm sure Stephen is going to give us an interesting sermon out of all that!' Marian smiled: 'It sounds to me as if you might be ready to become a preacher yourself, Christine,' she said.

'We still have work to do!' Alan pointed out. 'There are hymns to choose and prayers to think about.' 'The hymns will be difficult,' said Mollie. 'The only thing we really decided last time was that we couldn't choose hymns just because they are somebody's favourites.' 'Well, and that the opening hymn or songs ought to offer praise to God,' added Tom. 'I don't like the idea of the group choosing the hymns,' said John. 'Marian, why don't you choose them on our behalf? You are the musical one, after all.' 'Oh, but hymns aren't just about the tunes, they're about the words as well, and in any case, I don't play an instrument you know,' Marian replied. 'No, but you sing with the Circuit Choir and you have a pretty good idea of what our evening congregation can manage,' said John. 'Oh, very well – but you must give me a bit of guidance.'

So the housegroup spent a little while considering this. They eventually decided (i) that the worship would begin with two or three short praise songs from the supplementary song book the church had recently acquired; (ii) that they would say a Psalm of praise together after the opening prayers; (iii) that the hymn before the Gospel should be in praise of Jesus who gives us spiritual food; (iv) that the hymn after the sermon should be on the theme, and (v) that the final hymn or song could either be one which sent the congregation out in service of others, or which was particularly appropriate for the end of an evening service.

27

Marian made notes of all those things, and they were just about to move on when Tom said, 'Wait a minute; I think we may have a problem. Who is on the organ rota that night?' Julie did a quick reckoning. 'Let me see – if it's the third Sunday evening in the month, then it will be Arthur.' The members of the housegroup looked glumly at one another. 'Oh dear,' said Christine. 'I do hate to criticize, especially when I can't play myself, but he is so slow, and so limited in what he can play.' 'Yes,' said Julie. 'Do you remember a while back when a preacher chose that lively modern hymn of praise, "Tell out, my soul, the greatness of the Lord?" and Arthur made us sing it to the tune of "Abide with me"?' The group remembered only too well. The service had never really recovered after that. 'I do wish,' said Julie, 'that we could sometimes use another instrument than the organ. But I suppose we are stuck with it – and dear old Arthur – on this occasion. Marian, you will just have to make sure you choose hymns with tunes you know he will be able to play!' 'I suppose we could try putting it to him tactfully, that the opening songs will be modern ones, which he doesn't like, and ask if he would mind if Joan accompanied them on the piano instead,' said Betty. And they all agreed it was worth a try.

'What's left?' asked Alan. 'Just the prayers, I think,' replied Tom. 'I don't mind having a go at the Thanksgiving and Intercession,' said Mollie hesitantly. 'If you want me to, that is. I think I've got a fair idea now what should go in them. And I would put something in the Thanksgiving about our gratitude for the spiritual food Jesus gives us, and in the Intercessions about the church's work amongst the needy.' So that was agreed. 'I've never prayed in public before,' said John, 'but if Stephen would loan me some books of prayers I will try and find prayers of Adoration and Confession. I can read them during the week and alter them if I need to, so that they sound more natural coming from me.' That was agreed as well.

28

'Who is leading the service?' asked Christine. 'I think somebody should. I always find it off-putting when there are so many people taking part that nobody seems to be in charge.' There were murmurs of agreement, and a few moments later Alan found himself nominated.

Just when the group thought it had settled everything, Marian said, 'I know we're members of the congregation too, but have we really involved people in this service as much as we should have done?' 'Well,' said Betty, 'we could ask a couple of people to read lessons.' 'Yes, and you know how keen Andrew is on that music from Taizé,' said Tom. 'Couldn't we ask him to lead us in one of the sung responses during the Intercessions? They are so simple they don't need accompanying.' 'What a good idea,' (this was John), 'And I would like some opportunity to sit and meditate, or pray quietly. Joyce plays the flute – very well too. Why don't we ask her to play something short and meditative?'

So it continued for quite a while, as the housegroup members realized that the simple framework of the liturgy they had created gave them ample scope for calling on the gifts God had given to other people in the congregation. In that way they could help to make the service truly an offering of the people. Coffee, when it came, was nearly twenty minutes late, but Stephen still got his second cup!

Reflections

1. *The Importance of the Christian Year*

The service the housegroup were planning took place in the middle of July, on the 9th Sunday after Pentecost. Sundays described as 'after Pentecost' make up something like two-fifths of the year, and they are in what is sometimes called 'Ordinary Time', which means they are not in a special season of the Christian Year. In one sense therefore, it wasn't too important which lessons were read, or what the theme or mood of the service was. But Tom felt uneasy about Christine's suggestion from the previous week that they should read the story of John the Baptist. As he put it, 'We usually read about him on one of the Sundays before Christmas.' In recent years worship in many denominations has taken much more notice of the changing seasons of the Christian Year, which is good.

The real value of observing the Christian Year is that it makes sure that we celebrate the whole of the Christian faith on a regular basis. The Christian faith is a story, and we need the whole story for completeness. We also need the variety! After all, there is variety of mood and tone in our ordinary, everyday experiences. Human lives include funerals as well as weddings, and they have very different moods. This is true of Christian worship as well. Some parts of the Christian story move us to sadness and penitence. Others, to deep joy. The Christian Year ensures that these different notes are all sounded somewhere in our worship. Without it (and a Lectionary), it is possible for congregations to be subject to the particular likes and dislikes of those who lead its worship. Without it they may never hear, or have the opportunity of responding to, very important aspects of God's love: the story may remain incomplete.

Of course, every Sunday is a special day. An early Christian writer called it 'the eighth day of creation and the first day of the new creation' because it is the day on which Jesus was raised from the dead. Every Sunday, therefore, we celebrate the whole of the Christian Gospel. But the idea that some Sundays (and the days between) should be grouped together around certain festivals is a very ancient one. There is some dispute amongst scholars about exactly how the Christian Year originated, but it was virtually complete in the form in which we now know it by the fourth century after Christ. The various Christian traditions now follow the Calendar in slightly different ways, but its main features are constant. It is focussed around the two most important Christian festivals, Christmas and Easter. The other seasons lead us into and out of Christmas and Easter.

FOR DISCUSSION: How much of the Christian Year is usually observed in your church? What value do you find in it?

2. *The Shape of the Christian Year*

a. *Advent* begins four Sundays before Christmas. Its purpose is to prepare us for Christmas. St Paul tells us that 'when the fullness of time had come, God sent his Son, born of a woman' (Galatians 4.4). Advent has two main themes. Firstly, it reminds us of the various ways in which God's loving purposes have been at work in the past, preparing the way for the coming of Jesus. We think about significant moments in the story of our salvation, from the creation onwards. Secondly, there is the theme of expectation. We are living between the first and second comings of the Lord. In Advent we look forward to the time when God will bring in a new world of justice and peace. So the mood of Advent is penitence and expectation.

b. *Christmas* begins on Christmas Day and continues for twelve days. It is not just the celebration of a birthday. It marks the beginning of the fulfilment of God's saving purposes as we hail the coming of the Saviour of the world. So in the deepest Christian sense it is a time of joy and feasting. Scholars differ about why 25 December was chosen for Christmas. Some think that the Christian church simply took over a popular pagan festival in Roman times and turned it into a Christian one. But there is much to be said for the view that by early Christian calculations 25 December was the actual date of Christ's birth. In the Western world it has once again become a secular holiday. The Christmas story has caught the popular imagination. Because of commercial pressures, 'Christmas,' as somebody has said, 'begins earlier each year.' We may regret

31

this, but there is little we can do about it. Supermarkets will continue to play Christmas carols in November, whatever we say! But within the worship of the Christian community it is good to keep Advent properly, with our carol services and nativity plays as close to Christmas itself as is practicable.

c. *Epiphany* occurs on 6 January and is often celebrated on the Sunday after that date. Properly speaking, this is when the story of the Magi (Wise Men) is told, though they usually get mixed up with the Christmas celebrations! The theme of Epiphany is that the Light of the world has come in Jesus, and is now shown to all the world, so that all may live in that Light. Epiphany lasts just one day and brings the Christmas season to a close.

d. *Lent* is a period of 'forty days' with the addition of Sundays, preceding Easter day. It began as a time when candidates were trained for initiation into membership of the church through baptism, which often took place on Easter Day itself. As part of this training, they learned to repent of their sins and deny themselves, placing their whole trust in Christ who has defeated death. This theme still marks Lent today. Even people who do not attend church may ask, 'What are you giving up for Lent?' It begins on Ash Wednesday, when many Christians hold a special service of self-examination. On the Sundays in Lent we usually reflect on the journey of Jesus towards the cross. The mood of Lent is sombre: one of penitence and self-denial.

e. *Passiontide* is simply the last week of Lent. We often call it Holy Week. All of this time is focussed on the death of Jesus and the events that surrounded it. The final three days of Holy Week have always received special attention. It is now very common in all denominations to have services on Maundy Thursday, when the themes are the footwashing and the institution of Holy Communion. Also on Good Friday when in heart and mind we keep watch by the cross. Services of vigil, when we re-tell the long story of God's activity in human history, are becoming increasingly popular on Saturday. A late-night vigil may lead straight into the celebration of Easter itself.

f. *Easter* is the time of greatest rejoicing. Through the resurrection of Christ, God has fulfilled all that he promised. Sin and death have been overcome. The mood is of unrestrained joy, summed up in the traditional greeting and response:

> Alleluia! The Lord is risen!
> He is risen indeed! Alleluia!

Easter worship is full of Alleluias (the word means 'praise God'). This is even more effective if the ancient custom of having *no* alleluias during the whole of Lent has been observed! The Easter season lasts for fifty days, not just one! During that time the post-resurrection stories in the Gospels are explored and we rejoice in the transforming power of the resurrection in the whole of human life. Ascension Day comes in this season. The Easter season comes to an end with

g. *Pentecost*, which is also a festival in its own right. According to the Bible (Acts 2.1–13), the Holy Spirit gave power to the disciples to witness to the resurrection. At Pentecost therefore, we celebrate the Spirit's coming, to be with God's people for ever. Through the Holy Spirit's work the witness to the risen Christ continues today. It is through the Holy Spirit that our worship, indeed all our Christian living, is empowered and offered to God. The festival of Pentecost lasts one day.

FOR DISCUSSION: Which parts of the Christian Year do you find most helpful, and why? Are there any parts of it you would like to see more, or less, closely observed?

3. *When it's Not a Season . . .*

Worship offered during one of the special seasons of the Christian Year should reflect the general mood of the season. However, the service the housegroup were planning was not in a season, but on one of the Sundays 'after Pentecost'.

About three-fifths of the year is not in a special season. This also reflects the natural rhythms of life. There are times when we are sad and times when we are happy, but there are plenty of times when life is fairly routine. There are two stretches of the Christian Year not in a special season. One is after Epiphany to Shrove Tuesday (Pancake Day), the day before Ash Wednesday. The other is from the Monday after Pentecost to the day before Advent Sunday. It has been traditional to call these 'Sundays after Epiphany,' 'Sundays before Lent' and 'Sundays after Pentecost' (or, in the Anglican tradition, 'Sundays after Trinity).

In recent years the description 'Ordinary Time' has gained a wide currency and there is much to be said for it. The value of Ordinary Time is that it represents the normal and normative worshipping life of the Christian church. Sunday by Sunday the gospel of Jesus Christ is celebrated and lived out. God is to be found and glorified in the routine, as much as in the special times.

There are some special days, even within Ordinary Time! For almost half its existence, the church has celebrated the doctrine of the Holy Trinity on the Sunday after Pentecost. Trinity Sunday is a reminder (as we move into Ordinary Time), that the work of God, Father, Son and Holy Spirit, is at the heart of the Christian faith and the life of the church. An even more ancient festival is All Saints, which falls on 1 November. It is an occasion to give thanks to God for all that he has done in the lives of his people down the ages, not just in the lives of those who are referred to in some traditions as 'St'. Increasingly, congregations are using it to remember those who have died during the previous year. This is a useful pastoral ministry the church can offer, and it reminds us that all of us, living and departed, belong to the great communion of saints which is held in God's love.

Local churches also have their own festivals! In some Christian traditions there are local saints to be commemorated. Methodists tend to have Church or Chapel Anniversary, Men's Sunday, Ladies' Sunday and, of course, Covenant Sunday. Covenant Sunday is often placed at New Year, but can get mixed up with Christmas and Epiphany. Many churches now put it at the beginning of September. The other 'local festivals' each have their own character and importance, though they sometimes persist when they are no longer needed. It is not unknown for churches to have a Sunday School Anniversary when there has been no Sunday School for several years! Some Sundays are designated by a denomination for special concern, such as 'World Church Sunday' or 'NCH Action for Children Sunday', but these are for prayer and reflection within worship rather than festivals. In some cases worthy causes are commended, either ecumenically or by secular authorities. Again, these are subjects for prayer and reflection rather than themes for worship.

Ordinary Time then, is as important as the special seasons, for God is to be gloried in the whole of life.

FOR DISCUSSION: Do you think your local church has too many, or too few local festivals or 'special occasions'? Which are the ones your church values most?

4. *The Christian Year in Colour*

Worship is sometimes criticized as being too word-centred. We cannot do without words, of course, but some things can be better expressed in other ways. Beautiful flowers on Mother's Day or a Wedding Anniversary are a very eloquent way of saying, 'I love you.'

If worship is entirely about words, read, spoken or sung, it does not engage all our senses. One of the discoveries many churches have made in recent years is that simple coloured hangings and banners can do a great deal to enrich the worship we offer. Banners can help worshippers to reflect on the Christian story. They are a relatively inexpensive modern equivalent of the great stained-glass windows in mediaeval cathedrals and churches. In many churches people with fairly modest abilities have transformed the worshipping environment. Unfortunately, it is not unknown for banners to become as permanent as stained-glass windows. Care also needs to be taken that they are appropriate to the season. A banner depicting the empty tomb would be inappropriate in Lent, for example.

Pulpit falls and communion table runners can be made in seasonal colours and changed as the seasons change. Like the changing colours of the trees through the seasons of the natural year, this reminds us what part of the Christian Year we are in. Different colour schemes have been used by Christians in different ages and places. The following is a simple one which is widely used in churches of all denominations today.

a. *White or gold*. Used for festivals associated with Jesus: Christmas, Epiphany, Baptism of Jesus, the Transfiguration, the Easter Season, and All Saints.

b. *Purple*. Used for times of penitence and preparation: Advent, Lent, Passiontide (until the end of Maundy Thursday).

c. *Red*. Used for festivals associated with the work of the Holy Spirit: Day of Pentecost, commemorations of martyrs and Church Anniversary.

d. *Green*. Ordinary Seasons.

It is traditional not to use any colour, hangings or banners at all on Good Friday and Holy Saturday.

FOR DISCUSSION: Would you find it helpful if your church made more use of colour in worship? If so, how might this be done?

5. *Lectionaries*

The housegroup found itself in a little difficulty when it came to choosing the Bible readings for the service they were leading. Originally, Mollie thought they should choose a theme for the service and then find Bible readings to fit. It was Tom who worked out what was wrong with that. It would be, as he put it, 'like telling God what to say to us.' If, as we believe, the Bible is central to the life and worship of the church, then it must be allowed to speak to us in its own way. If we choose our theme or subject first and then look for readings to fit, we can be in danger of making the Bible say what we want it to say.

It is also possible, if worship leaders always choose their favourite readings, that quite a lot of the Bible goes unheard by the congregation. It is easy, then, for our discipleship to become distorted and one-sided. It can even happen that congregations end up hearing the same passages of scripture several times in a short period.

For these reasons, amongst others, the Christian church has usually found it useful to have a lectionary – a long word which simply means 'List of readings'. There is nothing sacred about any particular lectionary; thousands of them have been compiled over the centuries. There are *daily* lectionaries, useful

37

for private devotions and daily worship. The Prayer Handbook produced each year for Methodists in Britain and Ireland includes a daily lectionary. There are *Sunday* lectionaries, providing readings for public worship, and there are lectionaries which attempt the complicated task of being useful for either purpose.

Very broadly speaking, most lectionaries are compiled on one of two principles. They are either *thematic* or *semi-continuous*. Both these terms require some explanation!

Thematic lectionaries offer lessons with a common theme for each day. Semi-continuous lectionaries attempt to read straight through a particular book of the Bible on successive days. A strictly continuous lectionary would run into insoluble problems because major festivals of the Christian Year would have entirely inappropriate lessons allocated to them. Semi-continuous lectionaries, therefore, work on the principle of going straight through a book as far as possible, but taking material from elsewhere in that or another book for the seasons of the Christian Year. As can be imagined, compiling lectionaries is not a simple matter. Three of the many available lectionaries are of interest to British Methodists.

A. In 1967, an ecumenical body called the Joint Liturgical Group (JLG), produced a lectionary which was adopted by both the Anglican and Methodist churches. It was printed, with slight adaptations, in the 1975 *Methodist Service Book* and the 1980 Anglican *Alternative Service Book*. It operated over a two-year cycle and offered, usually, three lessons for the principal service of each Sunday or other special day. One of the lessons was called the 'controlling lesson.' It was, generally speaking, a thematic lectionary, and it offered titles for each Sunday. It was widely used and much valued. It was also criticized on the grounds that, being thematic, it tended to prejudge what the scriptures were saying to us. More serious, perhaps, was the feeling that it offered too narrow a selection of biblical readings, a number of which appeared more than once.

A further lectionary, supplying two lessons for a second service, was also produced by JLG, reflecting the themes of the lectionary for the principal service. This also appeared in the *Methodist Service Book*.

B. When the Roman Catholic Church produced a new lectionary it was widely admired. As a result, an ecumenical group known as the Consultation on Common Texts prepared a version of it which could be used by others. It became known as the *Common Lectionary* (CL). This has since been revised and published in 1992 as the *Revised Common Lectionary* (RCL). It operates over a three-year cycle, largely on the semi-continuous principle, though with thematic Old Testament lessons in Ordinary Time! So far as the Gospels are concerned, each of the three years is devoted to one of the Synoptic Gospels (Matthew, Mark and Luke) with John being interspersed.

C. In 1990 the Joint Liturgical Group published a revision of its previous efforts. This became known as JLG2 (and the 1967 version as JLG1). It was a very extensive revision. The cycle was increased from two years to four, thus including much more of the Bible. Only one set of readings was provided for each Sunday. It was suggested that if a second set was required, those for the same Sunday two years distant could be used. This was the suggestion the housegroup found useful. The titles and controlling lessons were dropped. The compilers attempted to keep a thematic link between the readings, though in the judgment of many they were only partly successful. They also introduced semi-continuous reading of the Gospels, allocating John's Gospel its own year. This lectionary was adopted, with some revision, by the British Methodist Conference to begin in 1992 with Year A.

A further Conference decision means that the lectionary will change again on the 1st Sunday in Advent 1998, when Methodism will move to the *Revised Common Lectionary*, only very slightly adapted.

FOR DISCUSSION: Do you know whether or not those who regularly lead the worship in your church use a lectionary all or most of the time? What might be the advantages and disadvantages for (a) a worship leader and (b) a congregation in always using the lectionary?

6. *Hymns in Worship*

The *Methodist Recorder* once carried a cartoon which depicted an elderly lady looking at a hymn-board on which were displayed the numbers of five unsingable hymns. The caption read: 'I told them when they went looking, never mind his degrees, look at his hymns.' As every worship leader knows, the choice of hymns is very important. Many worshippers will judge the effectiveness of a service by whether or not they know, or like, what they are asked to sing.

In the past, hymns have been more important in Methodist and Free Church worship than in some other traditions, though there are signs that this is changing. Anglican services, for example, have been largely built round the singing of psalms and canticles (this is especially true of Morning and Evening Prayer in the *Book of Common Prayer*). When hymns were introduced into Anglican worship in the nineteenth century, they were additional to the structure of worship, rather than an integral part of it. Methodism, on the other hand, was 'born in song,' as the Preface to the 1933 *Methodist Hymn Book* put it. The eighteenth-century Evangelical Revival, of which Methodism was an important part, produced many fine hymn writers. Amongst them was Charles Wesley, arguably the greatest hymn writer of all time.

Charles Wesley's hymns were written in order that the worshippers might learn about their faith. Since Wesley's hymns are saturated with biblical language they also, in the process, learned to love the Bible.

Yet in recent years what is sung in church has often proved controversial. In the second half of the twentieth century there has been an explosion in the writing of Christian songs and hymns. Modern technology has meant that this new material has reached ordinary worshippers more rapidly than ever before. No longer is it necessary to wait for the publication of a major new denominational hymn book. Supplementary books of new material, many of them produced on a non-denominational basis can now be found in many churches.

Variety of Christian musical resources is not in itself a new thing. For instance, it would have been possible for a worshipper in Britain in the 1880s to have attended an Anglo-Catholic service in the morning, a Gospel Hall revivalist meeting in the afternoon, and a Wesleyan Methodist preaching service at night. In the morning she would have sung a couple of 'office hymns' written centuries before and translated from the Latin, perhaps to traditional plainsong tunes written by monks. In the afternoon she would have sung some of the chorus hymns made popular by Sankey and Moody. In the evening she would have sung hymns by Charles Wesley and, probably, something by a then contemporary writer such as Bishop Heber from the 'New Supplement'. Even then, denominations were beginning to 'borrow' each other's hymns.

Such borrowing has continued and increased. It takes an expert to detect which denomination has compiled a new hymn book. When we also consider the proliferation of inter- and non-denominational books, it becomes evident that a huge variety of material is now available to every congregation. The tensions are perhaps unavoidable. What adds to them is that much of the new material is ephemeral and some of it is of poor quality. But there is nothing new about that! Most of Charles Wesley's hymns have not lasted. But, of course, it takes time to sort the wheat from the chaff. It is also often assumed (perhaps quite wrongly) that young people like only new songs, whilst older people like only traditional hymns.

So choosing songs and hymns for worship is possibly more difficult than it has ever been before. The housegroup was probably wise to delegate the job to Marian, not because it got them out of a difficulty, but because hymns chosen by groups often end up rather like horses designed by committees. At the same time, Marian was right to ask for some guidance as she set about her task. Those who choose hymns for worship usually bear the following in mind.

a. It is helpful if the hymns and songs express a variety of worshipping moods. At one point, Christine thought that the group should decide on a theme and then find hymns to fit it. If they had done that it might have made the service very dull and it would have deprived the congregation of the opportunity to voice other needs. So it was decided to have some songs of praise right at the beginning of the worship. Those nearest to the readings and sermon could be related to the theme. The final hymn could either be an 'evening' hymn (such as 'The day thou gavest') or one which carried forward the theme of Stephen's sermon.

b. It is helpful if there is variety in the length of the hymns and songs. If we are asked to sing five hymns, each with six verses and with eight lines in each verse, the worship will feel very heavy going. By the same token, four hymns or songs with only two verses apiece and four lines to each verse hardly has any impact at all on the worship.

c. It is helpful if there is variety in the style of the hymns and songs. Five Charles Wesley hymns will delight those who love them, but be less helpful to others. Similarly, five contemporary songs will appeal to some people, but leave others cold. In order that the Christian faith is given the widest possible expression in worship, it is good if some of the hymns come from other traditions and from other parts of the world church.

d. It is helpful if the choice of songs and hymns takes account of our musical capacities. Some churches know a very wide range of hymns, others a rather narrow one. Morning and evening congregations at the same church may be different in this respect. The housegroup was fortunate. They were planning worship for their own church, which they knew well. But it might be a mistake only to choose hymns which the congregation knows. Learning new hymns is one of the ways in which we can grow in our faith.

e. It is helpful to take account of the ability of those who will play whatever instrument is to lead the singing (and sometimes of the capacities of the instrument as well!). The housegroup was probably stuck with Arthur, and there would be no point in choosing something Arthur couldn't play. Or would there? There was a suggestion that, if they opened with some songs of praise Arthur would not want to play them. In that case, Joan could be asked to play the piano instead. Why could Joan not be asked to play for the whole service? Increasingly, the dominance of the organ is being questioned. Some churches have purchased electronic organs which are quite unsuitable to accompany singing of any kind. A good piano or a well-chosen keyboard is often seen as a better option. Even where the organ is a good one, other instruments may be found more suitable to accompany a wide range of contemporary Christian music. When we start to look we can sometimes be surprised by the range of musical abilities which exist even in relatively small congregations!

With all these factors to contend with, Marian may not have got it absolutely right! But she will have tried to help the worshippers to fulfil the biblical instruction: '. . . be filled with the Spirit, as you sing psalms and hymns and spiritual songs among yourselves, singing and making melody to the Lord in your hearts' (Ephesians 5.18b–19).

FOR DISCUSSION: What kinds of hymns and songs do you find most helpful in worship? Do you think everybody else in your church agrees with you? How can your church make sure that every worshipper is able to express his or her response to God through what is sung?

4

All-Age Worship

Naturally enough, the housegroup spent the first part of their next meeting reflecting on the service they had spent so long planning, and which had taken place the previous Sunday evening. On the whole, they felt quite pleased with themselves. Several people had said how much they enjoyed the service. They had even managed to persuade Arthur to let Joan accompany the opening songs!

'I feel we've done something worthwhile,' said Mollie. 'Perhaps we should offer to do it again sometime.' 'Why not,' said Tom. 'Or perhaps one of the other housegroups would like to have a go.' 'I can't help feeling,' commented Julie, 'that we got off rather lightly.' 'What do you mean?' asked Alan. 'Well for a start, we didn't have to do the sermon, Stephen did that. Also, it was an evening service. We're a much smaller congregation in the evening, mostly over forty. On the whole we know each other's likes and dislikes, what will work, and what won't.' 'I know what Julie means,' said Tom. 'It might have been different if we'd been tackling a morning family service.'

'I do wish we wouldn't call it that,' said Betty. 'Mrs Henson was talking to me after the last one. She said she's been a widow now longer than she was married, and they never had any children. She feels left out when it's called family service. I don't feel like that myself, because our children and grandchildren are usually there; but I can understand how she feels.' 'That's not really a fair thing to say though, is it?' asked Mollie. 'It doesn't mean the worship is only for people with families. It means that all of us together are God's family. Just on the one Sunday each month we worship together as a church family, instead of splitting up after the second hymn like we usually do.'

'You may well be right,' said Betty. 'But I don't think everybody sees it that way. We must be sensitive to their views as well.' 'Our new Superintendent seems to have picked that up,' said Marian. 'We used to have FS on the plan, meaning "Family Service"; now it has AAW, for "All-Age Worship". I do think it's a much better description.'

'I don't care what it's called,' said John, sounding quite angry. 'To be perfectly honest, I hate it. Last time I felt totally excluded; not because I'm single, but because there was nothing in it for me. It wasn't really worship at all. I've had just about enough of it. In future, when it's all-age or family worship, whatever it's called, I shall go somewhere else!' He took a deep breath. 'There now – I hadn't intended to say all that, but I'm glad I have. It's been on my mind ever since that service took place.'

There was quite a long pause whilst the others digested what John had said. Several of them had considerable sympathy with it. 'There wasn't a single decent hymn,' agreed Alan. 'We started with that silly little chorus when we had to sing the same words over and over again until we were sick of them. Then we had that thing on the overhead projector – something about thanking God for things that swim whilst we feed the ducks – goodness knows where they got that from!' 'It was from the material we'd been using in Junior Church,' said Julie. 'But I agree that it didn't work very well.' 'No, and the people at the back can't see the words on the overhead projector anyway,' said Betty. 'Well, they weren't missing anything in this case,' added Alan. 'And what about the Bible reading?' 'I can't remember what it was,' said Tom. 'That's hardly surprising!' Alan responded. 'It was read by Jenny Robinson. She's a lovely little girl, but she was ever so nervous. She rushed through it so fast it was just a meaningless gabble. When it came to the time for the address Mr Sims more or less had to read it again before he could talk about it.'

'I liked that prayer of Thanksgiving,' said Christine. 'It was a bright idea of Mr Sims to ask the children what they wanted to say 'thank you' for, and then make a prayer out of it.' 'Yes, but we couldn't hear it properly,' said Marian. 'That couple who started coming just before Christmas were in front of me, the ones with the young baby. The baby started to cry just as Mr Sims started to pray. I don't think anyone round me heard anything of the prayer. The mum took it out when we started singing, but it was a bit difficult for her because they were in the middle of a pew.' 'I remember what that feels like,' said Betty warmly. 'When I was a young mum it was not the done thing to bring young children into the service. There was a group of us who decided we would, but we had to put up with a lot of disapproval from some of the older ones. Every time our Paul made the slightest sound, old Miss Jenkins used to go "shush", very loudly. She made more noise than Paul.' The members of the housegroup laughed at Betty's recollection.

'At least it's not like that now,' said Christine. 'And I for one wouldn't want it to be. It must be right that the children are made to feel they belong, that the church is their spiritual home too, mustn't it?' 'I don't disagree with that,' said John. 'But, with respect, that's not really the point. Now take that prayer of Thanksgiving Christine mentioned. I agree that it was a very good idea. But why did Mr Sims only ask the children what they wanted to say thank you for? There were things I wanted to give thanks for, but the adults weren't asked. It wasn't all-age worship, it was children's worship. That's one of my grumbles.' 'I agree that's a mistake,' said Mollie. 'Some preachers seem much better at it than others and Mr Sims does struggle. Stephen usually does it quite well. I wish he could take all our family services but of course, with three churches to look after that isn't possible.' 'Those of our preachers who are teachers are best at it,' said Marian. 'I suppose they're used to dealing with the children.' 'That's not always true, Marian,' Alan responded. 'Do you remember that service Mrs Prescott took? It was like an old-fashioned RE lesson. I felt I was back in Sunday School!' 'Yes, old-fashioned is right,' said Julie.

'We do things differently in Junior Church these days. But Mrs Prescott didn't realize that. The Brownies and Cubs got really bored. Of course, it helps when worship leaders use the resource material we use in Junior Church. Stephen always does, and we send it to other people who are planned.'

'I'm not sure that it does help,' said John. 'Oh, I know it gives some continuity for the Junior Church, but it often makes it seem like an all-age Sunday School. I don't come to church for an RE lesson, however good. I come to worship, and increasingly I find I can't do it on those occasions.' 'Be fair, though,' said Mollie. 'Some of our preachers are brilliant at all-age things. June Barraclough and Mr Thompson, for example. They are just superb at keeping the children entertained.' 'Precisely my point,' said John. 'You've said it yourself, Mollie – entertained. I don't want to be entertained; I want to worship.'

Julie said thoughtfully, 'I suppose it's the sermon that's the real problem. When Sandra was our minister she just used to do one talk, about ten minutes, aimed at everybody who was there.' 'It didn't always work though, did it?' said Christine. 'No, but it was worth the try, and when it did work it was wonderful. We all ended up feeling that God had spoken to us,' Marian responded. 'On balance I think I prefer the way Stephen usually does it,' Betty said. 'A five-minute address aimed at the children, and then later on a seven-minute address directed at the adults. We enjoy listening to the children's address, and the children can just about keep quiet for seven minutes, so everybody gets something.' 'Yes, Stephen is quite good at that,' said Julie. 'Other people aren't as disciplined. I still shudder when I remember Ken Nicholson's attempt at all-age worship. He did a ten-minute talk to the children on Jonah and the whale, and then a twenty-five minute sermon on whether St Paul's views on women in church are still valid today!' 'That's just Ken Nicholson, I'm afraid,' Christine said sadly. 'There

48

are some people who ought never to be planned for all-age worship, and he's one of them.'

'I'm afraid you haven't convinced me,' said John. 'I agree that some people are better than others at leading all-age worship. I just don't think it ever really works. As for making the children feel at home – well of course we must do that. But surely that happens every Sunday? They are always with us for the first ten or fifteen minutes before they go to Junior Church.'

'Yes, but that's not always very satisfactory,' Julie replied. 'Not from the Junior Church's point of view. Sometimes we know the hymns and sometimes we don't. When it's communion the stewards usually forget to give the children the service orders, so they can't follow what's going on. And some preachers insist on giving a children's address.' 'I don't see what's wrong with having a children's address,' said Mollie. 'They are often very interesting.' 'I agree they can be,' said Julie. 'But they are hardly ever on the same subject we are using in Junior Church, and the children sometimes end up confused.'

'Goodness me, look at the time!' said Tom. 'I'd better put the kettle on. I know one thing though: I'm very glad it wasn't all-age worship we had to plan!'

Reflections

1. *Why Bother With All-Age Worship?*

John's dislike of all-age worship appears to run deeper than the issue of whether or not it is well done. In his view all-age worship is well-nigh impossible and ought not to be attempted. Other members of the housegroup, whilst not going as far as that, clearly find a lot of difficulties with it. Julie, who teaches in Junior Church, is also aware of the difficulties, but is sure that it is right to try. So is Christine, who argues that the children 'must be made to feel they belong'. All these sentiments, and more, can be found in most churches which hold all-age worship with any regularity. So how have we reached the position where this kind of worship is so controversial?

For most of the church's history all-age worship has been the usual way of doing things. Children and young people have been taught about the meaning and significance of worship simply by doing what their elders have done, as an accepted part of the church community. This is still largely true of some Christian traditions, for example the Orthodox and the Roman Catholic. Children have traditionally been expected to attend Mass along with their parents, without expecting any special concessions to them in the service. There have been changes to this practice in recent years, and in some parishes 'children's masses' have been instituted.

Simply taking the children and young people to what we would regard as an 'adult' service and expecting them to cope is not an option which is open to Methodists and others. For a start, our worship is too verbal and too cerebral. At most of our services there is a lot of talk and a lot of thinking, but not much to actually do, apart from standing up and sitting down in the right places and putting money in the collection plate. There is, in other words, not enough 'ritual'. Children are, in the main, enthusiasts for ritual. They feel comfortable doing things.

Similarly, with the exception of the Lord's Prayer, very little of our worship is repeated week by week. Prayers, readings, hymns and sermons all change, and there isn't much in Methodist and Free Church worship apart from those things! Children, on the other hand, like things which they can learn and join in saying. Those who have tried to change a familiar children's bedtime story and received the response, 'That's not how it goes, auntie,' will know what this means.

In other words, most of our normal worship is a very adult activity and offers very little to children and young people. In the past that has not seemed to matter very much. After all, the church provided them with their own activities through Sunday School and uniformed organizations. The Sunday School movement (which started in the eighteenth century) quite unintentionally laid the foundations for our present dilemma. Children were removed from adult Protestant worship, where they were no doubt very bored, and taken to special buildings to receive instruction and share in worship at a level considered to be more suitable for them. In many cases the Sunday Schools even met at a different time from church services. Sunday Schools have, of course, done incalculable good. But it is only in recent years that we have begun to appreciate the difficulties created by such an arrangement. There are two which deserve some reflection.

The first is that if children grow up having, literally, no experience of worship in church, it can be extremely difficult for them to make the transition from one to the other when they reach the age to finish in Sunday School. Worship in church appears to be a radically different activity from what they have been used to; as in one sense it is! Many of our churches have been deeply conscious that at that point of their development large numbers of young people are lost to the worshipping life of the church. Clearly, something needs to be done about that.

The second difficulty, which we have been slower to appreciate, is that worship for adults quickly becomes impoverished when they do it on their own. We come to think of worship as a very serious, cerebral activity. Children play, but adults work, we think. So worship becomes more like work than play. We squeeze out creative activities and refuse to admit that imagination has its part to play in our worship. Colour and symbol, dance and drama, mime and activity, are thought of as all right for the children, but not for the rest of us now we have grown up. In this way, though we have not always realized it, our worship becomes less rich and full than it might be. And, truth to tell, we forget that there are plenty of

51

adults who do not cope well with an hour of cerebral activity. Most of them are no longer around to remind us of the fact; they voted with their feet long ago.

There is also a deeper reason why keeping children and adults apart in worship is not a good thing to do. Worship is the activity of the whole Christian community. From the New Testament picture of the church as 'the body of Christ', we discover that, as Christians, we are incomplete without one another. By the same token, our private worship is incomplete. It is when we engage with God *together* that we offer worship in all its fullness. Now, who are the members of the body of Christ?

In the 1970s, well-meaning people, anxious to encourage the church to take children and young people seriously, coined the description, 'the church of the future'. Very quickly, others responded: 'No, they are not. They are the church of today.' Surely that is right? Part of the declaration in the 1975 service for the Baptism of Infants reads: 'By Baptism we receive this child into the congregation of Christ's flock . . . ' If we mean what we say, there can be no question but that our children are part of the body of Christ. Worship without them, therefore, is not worship by the full Christian community.

All-age worship is an attempt to experience what it means to worship together as the people of God. Nobody pretends that it is easy, but John was surely wrong to want to give it up as a bad job. The attempt must be made if the church is to be true to its calling under God.

FOR DISCUSSION: Do you agree with the argument that worship without children and young people is somehow incomplete?

2. *Children's Worship?*

John described a particular occasion as 'children's worship' rather than all-age worship. In that service, the worship leader asked the children and young people, but not the adults, for topics to be included in a prayer of Thanksgiving. John saw this as unsatisfactory. That preacher may not have been aware of it, but he was showing that he had not really understood the nature of all-age worship.

In some ways it is easier to lead something purely for the children than it is to lead an act of all-age worship. By continually focussing on the children, by keeping them busy and involved, in short by entertaining them, it is possible to get through an hour without too many mishaps. Whether anybody, including the children, will actually have encountered God in what has taken place, is perhaps another question, but one which needs to be raised. A 'successful' hour for the children may well keep a congregation relatively happy, at least on the surface. We are, rightly, conscious of our responsibility to present the Christian faith interestingly to our young people. Something which appears to keep them happy whilst in church has at least done some good, we feel. So, because we are grateful for that and don't want to seem ungracious, the question of whether anybody has actually worshipped may never be raised. Or at least, not until somebody like John finds that their deep dissatisfaction, even anger, can no longer be held back.

A mistake sometimes made in all-age worship is to patronize the children and trivialize what is happening. The basic needs of children in worship are exactly the same as the needs of adults. We all need to discover how wonderful God is, and how to offer our praise. We all need to reflect on the story of Jesus and give thanks for what he has done for us. We all need to think about our lives, to say sorry for the wrong things we have done and the good things we have failed to do, and we all need to know that God has made it all right, and we are forgiven. We all need to ask God's help in meeting the needs of others. We all need to be given the opportunity, through worship, to commit ourselves to the Christian way of life.

Obviously, the language we use, the way in which we express these things, varies with age and experience. But it would be a serious mistake to think that children are not capable of expressing these things through worship. They just need the opportunity to do so in ways which are appropriate for their particular stage of development – but that is true of adults as well.

We also sometimes assume that children and young people need to be shielded from the more difficult things of life. They cannot be, at least not any longer. For their own safety they now need to know about things which once upon a time adults would have kept from them. Perhaps they always did! Christian faith does not dodge the questions of evil, guilt and suffering. Indeed, they are at its heart. Yet we still sometimes assume that children cannot cope with these things and that, as a result, all-age worship ought to be unremittingly cheerful and bright! We may underestimate the young people.

Children often have a creative, if untutored, response to the central images of the Christian story. The challenge which faces us in all-age worship is to enable everyone present to engage with God through those images, and in ways which are appropriate and helpful. At times, language and imagery will need to be simplified – but not over-simplified!

FOR DISCUSSION: Think of some acts of all-age worship in which you have recently shared. How far were they truly all-age, and how far were they children's worship? How would you describe the difference?

3. *But What Do They Learn?*

One of John's grumbles was that all-age worship sometimes seemed to him more like an all-age Sunday School. This raises a very difficult question. What place is there in worship for what we might call Christian education? Julie mentioned the resource material that she and others regularly used in Junior Church. It was the custom at that church to send a copy of that resource material to those due to lead all-age worship.

Ecumenically produced material, called *Partners in Learning*, is widely used in churches of several denominations. Material published by the Scripture Union is also used on an ecumenical basis. The church the housegroup belongs to will almost certainly use one of these. Both offer a theme for the day, often as part of a series stretching over several weeks. This may, or may not, relate to the lectionary in use in the denomination.

Junior Church teachers find such resources invaluable. They offer material for worship, including songs to learn and prayers to say. They also offer material to help with the teaching, including stories, suggestions for visual aids and activities, notes on Bible passages and even suggestions for a sermon! The material is also sorted out into what is most appropriate for each age group within the Junior Church. All this is very positive, yet it also presents some problems.

Some worship leaders do not feel comfortable with using material of this kind. In some cases they may lack the skills or the imagination to use it well. Mrs Prescott, whose all-age worship was described as being 'like an old-fashioned RE lesson' was probably one such. Others are not at ease with being given a 'theme'. They prefer to work in their own way. Whatever the reason, if we try to use material which we have not been able to make our own, the result is likely to have a somewhat forced and inauthentic ring to it. On the other hand, if the material is not used at all in the worship, there will be a gap in the Junior Church teaching programme which they have to work hard to fill, especially if a series is in progress.

The greatest problem, however, comes in the way in which this material is sometimes used. It provides both worship and learning resources. The worship resources are usually fine for all-age worship. It is not always the case that the learning resources are equally appropriate.

If great care is not taken, an act of all-age worship can indeed become an all-age Sunday School, where the stress is on learning, rather than on the worship of God. It is quite understandable how this may happen.

Opportunities for teaching the Christian faith are limited. Few children seem to learn even basic Bible stories in school, for example. The chance to communicate something about the Christian faith, and what it means for our lives today, is a precious one. But worship and learning are not the same thing. Worship is the Christian community offering its life and needs *to* God, listening to God, meeting with God, and being changed and renewed in the process. Education is the Christian community talking *about* God, growing in its knowledge and understanding of God. The essential difference is that worship is offered to God, but teaching is addressed to the congregation.

Now, as soon as the distinction between worship and education is put like that, it appears much too sharp! There is an important sense in which we *do* learn as we worship. As we listen attentively to the scriptures being read, we learn something more about God's ways with people and his will for us. As we offer our hymns, songs and prayers, we are, as it were, thinking about our world, ourselves and God all at the same time. So we learn something about the relationships involved. If our worship is genuinely an engagement with God, then we grow spiritually. We become better disciples, our love for God and each other is deepened. In the deepest sense this is indeed a learning process. But it is learning which happens because we have celebrated our faith. It is very different from deliberately engaging in an act of Christian learning, important though that is in its own right.

It may seem as though this section has been rather negative. It is not intended to be. It is important that we are clear about the aim and purpose of what we are doing in all-age worship. When we have got that as right as it can be, other things follow naturally.

FOR DISCUSSION: Do you agree that there is a distinction between worship and education? If so, how would you define it? If worship is not to become an educational activity, what opportunities for Christian education (children and adults) might we need to create in the life of our church?

4. *Nuts and Bolts*

a. *Hymns and songs*

Since all-age worship is for both children and adults, there needs to be a mixture of hymns and songs with, ideally, something to which each age group can relate. Some churches find out what hymns and songs are sung in the local primary school and may therefore be known to the younger children. At the same time children must not be deprived of the heritage of Christian hymnody. If a classic hymn from what might be called the 'core repertory' of hymnody is included in each all-age service, they can begin to enter into deeper experiences of faith. For children, as well as for adults, singing words which you do not fully understand is easier than saying them!

If the worship resource material offers an attractive hymn or song, it might be possible to photocopy it or put it on the overhead projector. Copyright restrictions must be observed and if an overhead projector is used, it is important that everyone in church can see the words. Sometimes the children learn such an item in Junior Church the previous week, and then teach it to everyone else.

Many contemporary songs can be accompanied by something other than an organ! A good piano or keyboard is a boon for all-age worship. It is also possible to make use of the musical resources within the congregation. There may be some quite good instrumentalists around, adults and young people alike. It comes as a surprise to some people to discover how effective a hymn or song can be, when accompanied by, say, flute, clarinet and cello. This also enables more people to offer their skills in the worship of God.

b. *Prayers*
Because the needs of the worshippers are no different at all-age worship than on any other occasion, all the usual elements of prayer are included. It is helpful if prayers are kept relatively short, rather than trying to cover everything. Language may be kept as simple as possible, without being childish. This is not as difficult as it sounds! For example: 'Thank you for Jesus who died on the cross,' is better than 'Thank you for Jesus who was crucified.' On the whole, concrete language works better than abstract.

It is also useful to include responses during prayer in all-age worship. These are often printed on a notice or service sheet, but some cannot read. Short and easily memorized responses are useful, provided the 'cue' for the response is always the same, and easily recognizable. Some examples are:

. . . for all these things
Response: We thank you, Lord.

. . . loving God
Response: We pray for them.

. . . caring God
Response: Forgive us.

In the housegroup discussion, reference was made to the worship leader asking for topics to include in a prayer of Thanksgiving. This can also be done for Intercessions. It is important that the whole congregation, not just the children, are given the opportunity to respond. The person leading the prayers may need pen and paper. He or she must also be prepared for the unexpected. The present writer recalls a time when an enthusiastic walker in the congregation offered 'waterproof boots' as a topic for Thanksgiving! But why not? If worship is about the engagement of our lives with God, then that's fine.

There is also no reason why pre-written prayers cannot be farmed out to three or four members of the congregation, across the age-range of course. They can come to the microphone as a group and lead them. Intercessions work particularly well this way.

c. *Readings*

There is no getting away from the fact that some parts of the Bible make uncomfortable – even unsuitable – reading in all-age worship. There will be times when we judge that a particular passage just cannot be read because of its subject matter, but these will be rare. On the other hand, we must not assume that it is inappropriate to read a passage just because its subject matter is difficult. Some of the discourses in John's Gospel, or the more argumentative parts of Paul's letters, for example, might not be a first choice for all-age worship. Nonetheless, it is quite important that children as well as adults are exposed to them. Otherwise, children can grow up thinking that the New Testament consists largely of the parable of the Sower and the story of Zacchaeus. They need to know that there are things in the Bible to stretch understanding; things with which adults also wrestle. It is helpful if readings are prefaced with a brief sentence or two saying what they are about.

It is always good if members of the congregation are encouraged to read the lessons, and this practice has grown considerably in recent years. At all-age worship it is only right that the readers should be from various age groups. However, it must be admitted that there can be a problem with children reading in public. They should never be made to do so, of course, but even those who are willing to are sometimes nervous. Nervous adults tend to falter and stumble. Nervous children tend to rush and leave out punctuation marks, sometimes with disastrous results. 'Mary Joseph and the babe lying in a manger,' still surfaces at carol services! If children are asked to read, it is only sensible for a competent person to go through the reading with them beforehand. Some parts of the Bible lend themselves naturally to 'dramatic reading', with more than one voice. If properly prepared beforehand this can be very effective. Since there is no point in reading anything unless it can be heard, it goes without saying that readers of every age should be shown how to use the microphone.

FOR DISCUSSION: How many of the 'nuts and bolts' suggestions in this section have been tried at all-age worship in your church, and with what results? Can you think of other ways in which worship can be made genuinely all-age?

d. *The address*
The housegroup discussion revealed that there is more than one way to tackle this. The previous minister attempted just one address in the service, usually lasting about ten minutes. This is often considered ideal, but it requires very considerable skill. The gift of preaching to all ages simultaneously is not given to everyone. Even when it is well done, the attention span of the younger worshippers may not stretch that far.
There is something to be said for having two short addresses, one with the children largely in mind and the other mainly for the adults. If the one for the children is not childish, then it will

60

have something to offer to everyone. The older children, in particular, may benefit from the one which is mainly for the adults. The younger children can generally manage to keep quiet for a short time.

Preaching at all-age worship should be as varied as preaching at any other time. There is much to be said for a good story, especially a real-life situation. The Junior Church resource material is usually well-supplied with those. Of course, the aim is never to entertain, but always to proclaim the Christian good news.

FOR DISCUSSION: What kinds of addresses do you think work best in all-age worship?

e. *Creativity and spontaneity*

It is a fact of life that some people are more imaginative than others. It is also the case that some people need to have everything thoroughly prepared in advance, whilst others seem able to improvise on the spot. These things cannot be legislated for, but it is good to make use of the resources which are available.

Some churches have singing groups, or groups which perform liturgical dance. Both can enrich the worship, provided what is offered is integrated and not simply an 'item' from their repertoire, stuck into the service. It is sometimes rewarding if a biblical passage is acted out by a small group at the same time as it is read. Just occasionally, it will be appropriate for something to be mimed, possibly spontaneously.

Not every worship leader can create effective visual aids. If there is proper consultation in advance this can be done by other people.

One rule should always be observed: we should never applaud 'the young people' for singing, or reading, or dancing, or anything else they may do in the worship. It is patronizing, and young people experience it as such. In any case, when that happens we give the impression of one group performing to an audience, rather than a congregation worshipping to the glory of God.

FOR DISCUSSION: If there is to be creative participation in all-age worship, do you think this might call for a different way of preparing the worship?

5. *All-Age Every Sunday*

For many congregations a complete act of all-age worship only takes place on a monthly basis. Children may nevertheless be present for part of worship every Sunday. That part therefore needs to be of an all-age nature.

There are a number of ways in which Sunday morning can be used. Many people have commended a pattern whereby the children and adults meet separately for 'learning' sessions, then there is a break for refreshments, and finally the whole church family comes together for a time of all-age worship. Despite being widely commended, this seems not to have caught on. There is considerable resistance to extending our Sunday morning Christian activity beyond the hour we normally give to it.

In most churches, the pattern is for the children and young people to be present in church for the first ten to fifteen minutes, and then leave with their teachers for Junior Church. Though familiar, this has a number of drawbacks so far as the worship is concerned. Those elements of worship to which it is easiest to give an all-age character are prayers of Thanksgiving and Intercession, and the Offering. All these should really happen towards the end of the worship, as part of our response. If the children are in for the first part they get the impression that confession is the only thing Christians do when they pray. Sometimes there is a well-intentioned desire for them to hear a Bible passage before they leave. In that case they either finish up hearing only the Old Testament passage, or the Gospel ends up being read before the Old Testament, which is unhelpful. Sometimes there is a desire to take the collection before they leave. All these things pull the act of worship badly out of shape. Last, but not least, there is the unfortunate tendency for them to all sit together at the front, so when they leave there is a block of empty chairs or pews.

There is much to be said for doing things the other way round. If the Junior Church join the adult congregation either before or during the hymn after the sermon, this makes all-age worship much richer. It has the following advantages.

a. Brief information can be exchanged about what each group has been thinking about. This makes the whole congregation feel they belong.

b. Work which the children may have done in Junior Church can be brought and shown.

c. Prayers of Thanksgiving and Intercession can be properly all-age.

d. The Offering can be taken at what is the best place for it.

e. If the service is Holy Communion, the children are present for the most important part of it, which is the Prayer of Thanksgiving, and for the communion itself. Whatever the policy of a particular church about actually giving the elements to the children, this introduces them to the central act of Christian worship and ensures that the whole church family worships together at that point. It also enables the teachers to receive Holy Communion much more regularly.

It can also be noted, in churches which follow this practice, that it has an uplifting effect to see the church filling up rather than emptying! There is also some practical benefit in finishing worship together, which lessens any anxiety about young children being cared for after Junior Church until the service has finished.

A means of telling the Junior Church that it is time to return has, of course, to be devised. But this is usually not difficult.

The congregation in church has to get used to sitting for a few minutes whilst its other members come back in. That is a small price to pay for the chance of offering all-age worship, every Sunday, in the best way we can.

FOR DISCUSSION: What kind of pattern is followed in your church when only part of the worship is to be all-age? What are its advantages and disadvantages? What effect would a different pattern have on worship as a whole?

5

What about the Sermon?

The housegroup were somewhat relieved that they hadn't been given Sunday morning all-age worship to plan. If they had been, they would almost certainly have found it less frightening than they imagined, and probably very rewarding in the end. It was Julie who had pointed out that they had 'got off rather lightly,' as she put it, in another respect. Stephen had preached the sermon.

Christine found herself thinking about that from time to time. The next meeting was due to think about the housegroup's programme over the next few months. Christine thought that, before they started, she would briefly mention what was on her mind, just in order to clear it up. 'I've been wondering,' she said. 'If Stephen had asked us to be responsible for the sermon as well as the rest of the service, what would we have done? I don't think I would have had the courage to stand up there myself and preach. Would any of us? Or would we have decided not to have a sermon?'

'Well, honestly,' said Alan. 'I don't see why you should be afraid to stand up and preach, Christine. Or any of us, for that matter. Surely we couldn't do any worse than Mr Trent did on Sunday morning. He just went on and on about nothing in particular. There was no shape to it and it didn't go anywhere. I distinctly saw Edgar Anderson turn his hearing aid off – and I don't blame him!'

'Now, come on!' said Betty firmly. 'I can see what's going to happen if we aren't careful. We shall spend the whole evening criticizing the sermons we have heard recently, and that's not very constructive. In any case, I agree with Christine. I wouldn't have the courage to preach a sermon, so I don't want to criticize.' The housegroup thought about this for a minute or two, and then Marian said quietly: 'Thinking back, we were rather critical and negative when we discussed all-age worship.

Betty's right; we mustn't do it again, or it will become a habit. Why don't we try doing the opposite?' 'What do you mean, Marian?' asked Julie. 'An evening discussing what we like about the sermons we hear?' 'That might not take us very long,' Alan interjected. 'No, not exactly what we like. But what kind of sermons we find helpful, what subjects we value preachers dealing with – that kind of thing,' Marian continued. There were nods of approval from around the room. 'Come on, John,' said Christine. 'You're normally the quiet one, but you were very negative about all-age worship. Now's your chance to show us how positive you can be.'

John chuckled. 'Fair comment,' he said. 'What I really value in a sermon is being shown how our Christian faith makes sense in today's world. The people I work with know I'm a Christian. I don't mean I ram it down their throats or anything, but they do know. I get a fair bit of stick about it sometimes. You know the kind of thing I mean: people asking me whether I really believe that Jonah was swallowed by a whale. There's only one other Christian in the office and he isn't much help. He goes to one of those churches where they believe the Bible literally. He says, if the Bible said that Jonah swallowed the whale he'd believe that too. So I like the kind of sermons which help me to know what I believe. Yes, and how to stand up for it in ways which make sense to other people.'

'Hm,' said Betty. 'I follow what you're saying. I still remember that series of sermons Sandra preached on the Creed. I was amazed how many bits of my faith I'd never thought about before. I'd been saying the Creed for years, but that series of sermons really showed me how things fit together. I like a sermon from which I learn something I didn't know before; one which really gives me something to think about. Sometimes I think we'd do better not to have a sermon at all. We could have a video, or a discussion group like this one. But I do like that retired minister who comes sometimes – you know, the one who always quotes poetry in his sermons – Mr

Kerr, that's it. He preached a wonderful sermon about heaven. It must have been two or three years ago, but I can still remember it. Mind you, I don't always follow everything I hear. That sermon about the doctrine of the Trinity that we had recently from the Chairman of the District, for example. I'm sure it was very clever, but I couldn't follow much of it.'

'No,' said Mollie. 'I'm afraid I told him after the service that it had all been a bit above my head.' 'Mollie, you never did!' said Marian. 'Whatever did he say?' 'He just said, Jump!' Mollie replied. The group dissolved into helpless laughter. When they had recovered themselves, Mollie continued: 'The kinds of sermons John and Betty seem to like haven't always got enough Bible in them for me. Like that series of Sandra's on the Creed. It was very good and I learned a lot from it, but there wasn't much biblical material in it. Since I came to know the Lord, reading the Bible has taken on a whole new meaning for me. The Bible is where I meet with my living Saviour. I really like sermons which are properly based on the Bible, especially those that explain all the difficult bits. Now Stephen is very good at doing that. Remember that sermon he preached from the Letter to the Hebrews, the one on Jesus as the great High Priest? That was really wonderful. I'd read that bit several times before, but never made much of it. It even turned up in my Bible reading notes last year, but I still couldn't understand it. Stephen's sermon really explained it to me, and I went away wanting to praise the Lord for his wonderful salvation.'

'Yes, that was a good sermon; one of Stephen's best,' said Tom. 'But sermons on the Bible aren't always like that, are they? There was that awful one from Mr Harrison. He just told us everything he knew about the Hivites and the Jebusites. It sounded as if he was reading out of a Bible dictionary.' 'Now dear,' said Betty. 'We're starting to get grumbly again!' 'I know, I'm sorry,' said Tom. 'But really, what help is that to anybody? No, the sermons I most appreciate are those which help us to cope with life's problems. Oh, I don't mean the trivial little things that happen every day, but the big things. When our Paul died I don't think I properly heard what any preacher was saying for months afterwards. I just couldn't concentrate. But then, one Sunday evening, we had a preacher from another circuit on whatever it's called – Local Preacher's Sunday, I think. I can't remember her name, and I don't really remember her sermon in any detail. But I know she talked about how being a Christian didn't protect you from the bad things in life. That made me sit up and listen. And she went on to say that because Jesus experienced suffering and death we could know that God shares our pain. There was more as well, I think. But that was enough for me. Betty and I had been struggling, but that helped us to cope. Ever since then, I have really valued sermons that don't offer simple answers.'

There was a silence: the group had a deep respect for how Tom and Betty had dealt with their personal tragedy. Then Marian said, 'I agree with all that Tom said. I felt much the same way after Brian died. One of the things which took a long time to come back after I was widowed, was the ability to pray. I wanted to say my prayers, but I found I couldn't. Or if I did manage to mumble my way through some, they didn't seem to mean very much. I found a lot of help from sermons which taught me how to pray again. We don't get many of them. But you can always rely on that nice Mrs Scott, you know, the one who sometimes organizes Quiet Days for the circuit. She has a kind of stillness about her when she leads the service. I always feel helped just by listening to her. I hope it doesn't sound a silly thing to say, but I always feel God is a bit closer when Mrs Scott preaches. You can tell she's a woman of prayer. Sermons like the ones she gives us have taught me how central prayer and worship is to my faith. As you know, I've always been a Martha rather than a Mary. I like to be involved in things. But since Brian died I've learned that my life needs a still centre. That's where the strength to be doing comes from. It's Mrs

Scott, and people like her, who preach the sermons that help me most.'

'Oh, goodness!' said Christine. 'You all know what you like, don't you? I'm not sure that I do. I just like a good sermon, and I know what I mean by that when I hear one. I don't think I'm as bothered as some of you are what it's about. Like Mollie, I enjoy a sermon based on the Bible, when it's interesting. I appreciate having my faith explained to me, like Betty and John do. I agree with Tom that a sermon should help us cope with life's problems. I wouldn't think much of a sermon which didn't have something of that about it. I'm not sure, Marian, that I want to hear lots of sermons on prayer, though my prayer life could do with some help. No, I just like a good sermon, whatever it's about.'

'Yes, but what do you mean by a good sermon?' asked John, genuinely interested. Christine thought for a bit and then said, 'For me, a good sermon has a sense of where it's going. They don't all; some of them just ramble aimlessly. I like to feel as if I'm being taken on some kind of journey in a sermon. And I like it to have, oh, I don't know quite what to call it – life and vitality I suppose. I can't cope with sermons like that one from Mr Harrison on those ancient tribes or whatever it was. They are like the essays we had to write in school. There's no real life in them. A good sermon makes me feel that faith in God is a living thing which actually matters.'

'I entirely agree with that last bit,' said Alan. 'Thank you for saying it, Christine, love. Now me, I'm a "tell me the old, old story" man. I don't like it when preachers come up with some new theory about how Paul or James or John really meant something quite different from what we've always thought they meant. Too many sermons, in my opinion, get away from the real centre of the Christian faith, which is the story of Jesus. Now I need to hear that story – for the reasons given in the hymn. I know it so well, but I often forget what it means. And I know that I need frequent reminders of how Jesus

69

is my Saviour. That's the only real comfort I know. "Christ Jesus makes thee whole" – that's what I want to hear from preachers. In Bethesda – the chapel Christine and I used to attend before they closed it – there was a note in the pulpit where preachers could see it. It read: "Sir, we would see Jesus." That's the kind of preaching I want – the kind that shows me Jesus and tells me the old, old story of his love for me.'

'I like sermons that tell me the story,' said Julie. 'I'm not an intellectual, and I know I get bored fairly easily. But Alan, it isn't enough for me just to hear the story of Jesus, even though it's so wonderful. I suppose you have a much more mature faith than I have – after all, you've been a Christian a lot longer. I need the connections spelled out for me. I need help to understand *why* the story of Jesus still matters, and what it has to do with my own life, day by day. Now the preacher whose sermons really ring bells with me, is the Superintendent. He's always telling stories about people and about real-life situations. Sometimes he tells a Bible story as though it was happening today. I can put myself into those, and I can understand them. I'm always pleased when I see he is down to preach. I know I'm going to come away feeling that it's good to be a Christian. I'm afraid I don't always understand those sermons which try and "explain" Christianity to me – sorry, Betty, not even Sandra's series on the Creed, even though you thought it was so good. Maybe I'm simply not clever enough for sermons like that. But a good story helps me more than I can say.'

The housegroup lapsed into silence for a few moments. Then Marian said, 'I'm ever so glad I had the idea of discussing the things we value most about the sermons we hear! I think it's been one of the best evenings we've ever had. Oh, and can I just remind everyone that there is no service on Sunday evening at our church? It's the Week of Prayer for Christian Unity, and we've all been invited to St Mary's for the evening service. It's at 6.30 p.m., don't forget! Now Tom, are you going to put that kettle on?

Reflections

1. *In the Beginning Was the Sermon*

We are all critical of sermons sometimes. From time to time people are critical about the very idea of preaching. Is it an appropriate way of sharing the gospel today? A cartoon once depicted an incredibly high pulpit, with many steps leading up to it. All that could be seen from the pews was the top of the preacher's head. The caption read: 'My subject today, is Communication.' In the days when pulpits were, in general, higher than they are now, preachers were sometimes described as being 'six feet above contradiction'. In an age of television, videos and home cinema, there can appear to be a remoteness about preaching. In an age of 'sound-bite' politics, probing interviews and sometimes intrusive questioning, the idea of one person talking for even fifteen minutes, seems dated. We are not the first generation to find this a problem. Seventy years ago a clergyman described preaching as 'like trying to fill a row of milk bottles from a watering-can'. How has it come about that preaching has been a central part of the worship for Christian people down the centuries?

The answer to that goes back to the beginnings of the church. Some time after the resurrection of Jesus, when his disciples were together in one place, the Holy Spirit came upon them. The immediate result was that Peter delivered a sermon (Acts 2.14–36). The Holy Spirit gave the Christian community a message to proclaim and the courage to proclaim it. That sermon was preached to unbelievers. The result, according to Luke, was that 'those who welcomed his message were baptized, and that day about three thousand persons were added' (Acts 2.41).

71

Acts 3.13–26 tells how Peter preached to an astonished crowd following the healing of a lame man. Acts 4.8–12 records Peter, not just explaining the healing which had taken place, but again proclaiming the lordship of the risen Christ. Much the same thing happened when the apostles were being interrogated about their activities (Acts 5.29–32).

Those sermons were delivered in Jerusalem in the earliest days of the church's life. Acts 10.34–43 tells of what happened when Peter was directed to the household of Cornelius. Again, he preached a sermon about the risen Christ. This was the first occasion on which the Christian message had been preached to people who were not Jews.

Just as the first result of the Holy Spirit's coming upon the disciples was that Peter preached, so the first result of Saul's conversion on the road to Damascus was that he began to proclaim Jesus (Acts 8.20). Luke's description of what such a sermon might have been like is in Acts 13.17-41. On a number of occasions Acts refers to preaching activities usually, though not always, resulting in conversions and the founding of new churches.

Most of the preaching referred to in Acts is, of course, directed towards those who had not heard the Christian message. Paul summarized what his own preaching had been about, when he defended himself before King Agrippa (Acts 26.20). There are fewer references to what preaching might have been like at Christian worship. Acts 20.7–9 records that Paul, preaching at worship, went on so long that an unfortunate young man went to sleep and fell out of the window! Later, we have a 'pastoral address' from Paul to the leaders of the Ephesian church (Acts 20.18–35).

Biblical scholars differ about whether the sermons recorded in the Acts of the Apostles would have been preached as they are now written down. It may be that Luke has given us summaries of what was said, or has written them up in his own style. That need not worry us. From this brief look at the Acts of the Apostles we can see that preaching itself was central to the life of the Christian church from the very beginning. It was the means through which the faith was spread. It was also a way in which the new believers were built up in their Christian faith.

It is a pity we do not have more examples of sermons preached to Christian believers. Some scholars think that preaching or teaching material underlies some of the New Testament letters, such as I Peter and James, but we cannot be sure.

FOR DISCUSSION: Why do you think God chose preaching as the earliest way of sharing the Gospel? Does this bind us to continue with preaching today?

2. *Why Do We Still Preach?*

Whilst preaching was appropriate and right for biblical times, that does not entirely explain why the church has gone on doing it!

At the risk of oversimplifying, it can be said that preaching reflects the pattern of God's communication with the human race since almost the beginning of the biblical story. God sends people, with a living message. So, for example, God used Moses, not just to deliver his people from slavery, but to give them a way of life in accordance with his will. The Torah (which we usually call the Law of Moses) was, of course, written down, studied and explored. But it came initially through God's chosen person. From time to time in Israel's history, God raised up prophets, such as Elijah, Jeremiah or Hosea. Many of these had their words written down, or wrote themselves. But the message came initially through the words, and sometimes the deeds, of the prophet. The same is true in New Testament times of John the Baptist. Through these messengers, God gave himself in love, called people to account

73

for their misdeeds and offered them reconciliation with himself.

Christians believe that with the birth of Jesus something even more amazing happened. At the Incarnation God did not send yet another messenger, he came himself. Jesus not only brought the message – he was the message. In his person, and by his words and deeds, God made his fullest communication with human beings. After his death and resurrection the Holy Spirit came upon the disciples. The result was a living message. If we look closely at the preaching of the disciples, we will see that the story of Jesus, crucified and risen, is always at the heart of that message. God still offers people a relationship with himself, but it is now through Jesus.

This is something the world needs to hear. When Paul writes: 'And how are they to hear without someone to proclaim him?' (Romans 10.14), it might seem that he is asking a simple practical question. After all, television, radio and printed books did not exist in his day! There is more to it than that. The message is that God is personal, has made himself fully known in a human life and still reaches out in love to other human lives. So the means by which the message is brought has also to be personal. God goes on doing what he has always done – using people through whom to speak to his world. Ordinary, frail human beings are – usually to their utter astonishment – the means by which God speaks to other ordinary, frail human beings of his inexhaustible love. The great Sri Lankan Christian, D. T. Niles, once defined evangelism as 'one beggar telling another beggar where to find bread'. It is true of all Christian preaching.

FOR DISCUSSION: Do you agree that because God's message is personal, the means by which it is brought must also be personal?

3. *What is Preaching all About?*

Books on preaching sometimes offer the advice that every sermon should have an 'aim' and that this should be clear in the preacher's mind before the sermon is written. Alan's comment about Mr Trent's sermon is a reminder that not every sermon achieves this! Is there an 'aim' for preaching as a whole? Is there something which every sermon, no matter what its topic or occasion, should always be designed to do?

If we look in detail at the New Testament preaching, we find that certain elements keep occurring. These are referred to by biblical scholars as the *kerygma* (pronounced 'kerugma', and from a Greek word meaning 'herald'). They are:

a. God has fulfilled the promises he made in the past through the prophets.

b. The fulfilment has come through something which has recently happened, the life and ministry of Jesus of Nazareth.

c. The life and ministry of Jesus culminated in his death and resurrection. There God is to be seen at work. More, God has not only raised Jesus from death, he has 'exalted' him. Jesus is not only the promised Jewish Messiah, he is also Lord of the whole universe.

d. The Holy Spirit has now been poured out upon God's people.

e. In the light of all this, those who hear should repent of their sins, receive God's offer of forgiveness and the Holy Spirit, and be baptized.

Clearly, all this was designed to enable the hearers to encounter God, by responding to what he had done in Christ. At the heart of Christian preaching is the telling of the story of what God has done in Jesus Christ.

Alan was quite right to say that preaching which showed him Jesus and told him the 'old, old story' was preaching which kept close to the centre of the Christian faith. In an important sense this is the aim of every sermon.

But Julie made an important point. Just repeating the story baldly is not in itself good preaching. As she put it, she needed help to understand *why* the story of Jesus still matters, and what it has to do with her daily living. Christians have always experienced that need, and there is evidence of it from the earliest Christian communities. As well as the *kerygma* we find *didache* (pronounced 'didakay', a Greek word meaning 'teaching'). Examples of this can be found in the New Testament letters and elsewhere. But this is not teaching in the sense of imparting information. Rather, it is the process of unfolding what it means to believe in the *kerygma*. If we do indeed put our faith in Jesus crucified and risen, and repent of our sins, what are the implications of that for who and what we are?

Perhaps the clearest example of all this is found in the letter Paul wrote to the church in Rome. In the first eleven chapters we find Paul's most comprehensive, and difficult, exploration of the nature of the Christian faith, concluding with a great outburst of praise to God. He begins the next chapter with the words: 'I appeal to you therefore . . .' and the rest of the letter is largely about practical Christian living. Perhaps that is what early Christian sermons preached to believers were like: first the unfolding of what the Christian Good News was all about, then the practical consequences of it.

The aim of all preaching then, is to begin, maintain, strengthen or explore, our relationship with God. Or, as John Wesley put it: 'To invite. To convince. To offer Christ. To build up; and do this in some measure in every sermon.'

FOR DISCUSSION: Do you agree that the aim of all preaching is the one suggested in this section? If not, what would you put in its place?

4. *Variety in Preaching*

John most valued sermons which helped him make sense of
Christian faith in today's world. In the process they gave him
some ammunition to fire as he contended for the truth of
Christianity in a hostile working environment. That kind of
preaching is sometimes called 'apologetic'. The word might
suggest that we ought to apologize for what we believe. Of
course, it does not really mean that at all. Apologetic preaching
argues the case for the faith we hold. John did not feel his
Christian colleague, who is content simply to quote the Bible,
helps him very much. Now it is true that Christianity is a
revelation from God, and the story of that revelation is
contained in the Bible. But since we are thinking beings, we
need to know that what we are being asked to believe is
actually believable, not simply absurd nonsense. Apologetic
sermons help us to do that. The sermon Paul preached in
Athens (Acts 17.22–31) is of a quite different character from
anything else he preached. This is because his audience was
different. Instead of beginning with the Jewish scriptures –
whose authority they would not have accepted – he began with
the religious beliefs of his audience. From there he moved to
some general truths about God, and ended with the reference to
Jesus and the resurrection. It was an apologetic sermon. In a
contemporary Christian setting, such sermons help us to give a
reason for the hope that is in us (I Peter 3.15). As we listen to
them, we can see how they help to make our engagement with
God lively and thoughtful.

Betty liked a sermon from which she learned something –
provided it was not too difficult. She had particularly valued a
series of sermons their previous minister had preached on the
Creed. This kind of preaching is sometimes called 'doctrinal'.
It explores the meaning and significance of what Christians
believe about God. If well done it will inevitably have some
'apologetic' content. Doctrinal preaching sometimes seems

intellectually demanding, or difficult to understand. It need not be, but it does not always hurt us to be stretched a little. The Holy Spirit has been active in the lives of thousands of great Christian thinkers over the last two thousand years. That is part of our heritage. As we listen to doctrinal preaching we can find our engagement with God made deeper and richer.

Mollie was clear that she liked sermons which were firmly based on the Bible. The subsequent discussion was a reminder that it is possible for a sermon to sound biblical, but actually do little more than relay information we could find in a Bible dictionary. That of course, is not biblical preaching. Some preachers are gifted at preaching on a biblical passage, explaining what it is all about. This is called 'expository' preaching. Many of us are like Mollie; we are grateful for help in understanding what the Bible says – especially the difficult bits. There is more to expository preaching than explaining the background to the passage, or the meaning of the words in which the Bible was originally written. Such things are only the beginning. If there is nothing more, we do not have preaching, we have an essay on the Bible. Good expository preaching connects with the world in which we live, work and suffer, so that biblical truth becomes something by which we can live. As we listen to expository preaching we can be helped to build our engagement with God on firm foundations.

Help to cope with the problems of life was what Tom valued in a sermon. He didn't mean well-intentioned advice about daily living. What he sought were insights into how Christian faith provides help with the difficult things. Preaching which begins from where we are is sometimes called 'situational' preaching. We may note, too, that Tom was not necessarily looking for simple answers, or indeed answers at all. His own particular need had been the sudden death of a much loved child. Illness, suffering, death and bereavement are part of our humanity. There are no 'answers' to them. But Christian faith is rooted in the *kerygma* which has suffering and death at its heart, but not as the final word. This speaks to the human condition of a God who is involved with us in what we go through. As we listen to situational preaching we can experience the grace and presence of God related to our everyday situations.

Julie also liked situational preaching, but she especially valued 'stories about people'. This kind of preaching often has an element of 'testimony' about it. That is an ancient element in Christian preaching. Paul gave his testimony about how he had been converted on the road to Damascus (Acts 22.3–11). In the Methodist and Free Church preaching tradition, testimony to what the Lord has done for the preacher has been a strong element. In Roman Catholic preaching, telling the story of what God has done in the lives of the saints of the church has been equally prominent. It has its dangers: it may become repetitive and stereotyped. If not well done, it can draw attention to the preacher rather than to God. The greatest danger is that it can suggest that unless the hearers have had the same kind of experience as the preacher (or St Paul), they are not real Christians. But well done, listening to the story of God's grace in a particular human life may encourage the rest of us to allow God's grace to get to work in us as well.

Marian valued what we sometimes call 'devotional' preaching. After her bereavement, her need was to learn to pray again. Sermons which encourage us to become more proficient in prayer, to read our Bibles more faithfully or to offer our worship more sincerely, can be a great help. They may become rather narrow, as if Christian faith was only about 'me and God', ignoring others and the world around us. But Marian didn't value them for that reason. As an activist, always involved in things, she knew the need for what she called a 'still centre'. That is an important lesson to learn in a world (and a church) which is often frantically busy. Since it is through worship and prayer that we make the things of God our own, hearing devotional preaching may help us to keep close to God who is the source of our strength.

The list of sermon types the housegroup came up with is by no means exhaustive; many more could have been added. There are 'social issue' sermons, which may highlight particular issues of social concern in community or nation. They can run the danger of making us feel guilty about something we can do little or nothing about. But they are needed because they help us to see that the Lordship of Christ is over all the world. There are 'ethical' sermons, which deal with how Christians should behave in relation to particular moral dilemmas (human sexuality, drug abuse or honesty at work, for example). These are difficult things to preach about, and the danger is always of untrue generalizations. At their best they help us to engage with a God who wants only the best for us and for our world.

It is fairly obvious that most sermons are a mixture of many of these things!

It was Christine who seemed genuinely to appreciate all sorts of sermons – provided they were good ones! Pressed to say what she meant by a 'good' sermon, she struggled a bit. But she knew a good sermon when she heard one, not least if the structure was clear. Her final comment was that a good sermon made her feel that 'faith in God is a living thing which actually matters'. In other words, a good sermon is one which helps us to engage with God, no matter what subject it is on.

Christine was essentially right. It is to be hoped that we hear many good sermons, but we will never hear a perfect one. Preachers never cease to be amazed that God has called them to such a task, because they also know their unfitness for it. As has been said: the best thing a preacher can do is not get in God's way too much.

As we listen to sermons we need to pray for the preacher and for ourselves. The prayer should be that as we hear the words of a fallible and sinful human being, we nevertheless meet with the living God and hear his word for our lives today (see Luke 10.16).

6

What Is Worship All About?

There was a good deal of chatter as the housegroup assembled for the final meeting of that series. 'I can guess what we are all talking about,' said Betty. 'It's last Sunday evening's service at St Mary's, isn't it?' They all readily agreed that it was. The local Churches Together had decided that on the Sunday of the Octave of Christian Unity, congregations would take it in turns to host the service. These were not to be ecumenical services as such. Rather, each church would hold worship in its usual style and invite others to experience worshipping in that particular way.

On this occasion the worship had been at the Parish Church of St Mary the Virgin. St Mary's was a very old-fashioned Anglican church which still used the 1662 *Book of Common Prayer* for most of its services. What the group had attended, along with other Christians from the area, was a traditional Evensong.

'It did me a power of good,' said Marian. 'My grandmother was Church of England and I used to go with her to Evensong when I was a child. It all came back to me. There was something very familiar about it, and I really enjoyed it.' 'I'm afraid I didn't,' said Tom. 'I've never been to anything like it before, and I found it terribly dull! I only knew one of the hymns, and in any case hardly anybody was singing.' 'That's true,' said Alan. 'And we could hardly have joined in the Psalms and those other things – Canticles – because we didn't know them. I think we were just expected to listen to the choir.' 'They are a very good choir,' Betty commented. 'I didn't mind not joining in. They sang a lovely Anthem, and sometimes I like to worship by just listening.' 'There was nothing lively,' complained Mollie. 'And all that quaint language – thees and thous and things. I struggle with those sometimes in hymns, but they don't stand out as much when you're singing. It made the

81

prayers seem unreal. I hardly managed to praise the Lord at all.'

'Not all Anglican churches are like that though, are they?' Christine asked. 'Some friends once took Alan and me to the one they go to. They didn't even use a book. They sang a lot of choruses and modern songs, and people clapped and raised their hands in the air.' 'Oh, that's wonderful,' Mollie enthused. 'You really know the Holy Spirit is at work when you go to a place like that. It's as if everybody really wants to praise God with their whole being.' Alan snorted. 'I thought it was terrible,' he said. 'And the worst bit was when someone spoke in "tongues" as they call it. Christine and I couldn't understand a word. I don't see why the Holy Spirit has to be noisy or unintelligible. I like worship to be dignified, orderly and quiet.'

'If you like it quiet, Alan, you should go to a Quaker meeting,' said John. 'I went once with a friend. We sat in almost total silence for an hour. Only one person spoke and there didn't seem to be a leader. It was a strange experience, though by the end I thought I was getting the hang of it.' 'Oh, I couldn't worship like that either,' said Alan. 'I would miss my hymns too much.' 'Brian and I went to a service in Germany once, when we were on holiday,' Marian chipped in. 'We thought it would be like what we were used to, but it wasn't. They sat down to sing and stood up to pray! And they only sang one hymn. It had about twenty verses and they sang it in four or five bits.'

'That's nothing to the service we once went to in Greece,' said Tom. 'Do you remember that, Betty? The whole church was full of little pictures and people were kissing them. The air was full of incense and they kept ringing bells. We didn't know what was happening most of the time, and of course, it was all in a foreign language. Some of the service took place behind a screen and the priests kept coming in and out in their heavy vestments. Now that really was an experience!'

'It sounds a little bit like a service I went to when my nephew was christened,' said Julie. 'That was in a Roman Catholic church. They had vestments and incense and candles and bells and things. But most of the time I could understand what was happening. The service wasn't really very different from the christenings we have at church, except that the sermon was so short I almost missed it.'

'It's a bit strange though, when you think about it,' said John reflectively. 'If we are all Christians, why do we worship in such different ways?' 'Habit, and perhaps temperament, I guess,' answered Betty. 'No, but John's right,' said Christine. 'After all, some of the differences are very big. If I was a visitor from Mars,' she went on, 'and I went to services in all the different churches, I might think they were all different religions. In one church there would be candles and incense and lots of colour and vestments, and in another, none of those things. In a Salvation Army Citadel there would be enthusiastic singing and a band, and in a Quaker Meeting, silence. Some places would use several books, others none at all. I don't think I'd realize all these different places were Christian.'

'So, what is worship all about?' asked Betty. 'Take the service we planned a few weeks back. We learned a lot about what goes into an act of worship. We did our best to plan something which would help everybody who was there to put something in and get something out. But if there had been a visitor from that church in Greece that Tom and I went to, it wouldn't have been very satisfying for them, would it?' 'Perhaps not,' said Alan. 'And I am still wondering whether we have ever answered those questions which Julie asked arising out of her story about her friend, Fiona. Why do we worship, and what does it achieve?' 'Oh, I don't know,' John responded. 'I think we've learned quite a lot about that along the way, probably more than we realize.'

'I think you're probably right,' said Marian. 'Anyway, we've just got time to decide what we are going to discuss in the next series, before I make the coffee.'

Reflections

1. *The Problem of Variety in Worship*

The housegroup's experience in attending a sung Evensong at St Mary's prompted reactions which we may well have shared when going to worship of a kind we are not used to. Some things, though unfamiliar, help us to worship. Other parts of the service are not so helpful, either because we do not understand them or because they happen to make no appeal to us.

Increasingly, this is becoming an issue within Christian denominations, and within individual churches. At one time, a worshipper attending a service in a particular denomination knew more or less what to expect. Nowadays it is not so simple. It is quite easy to find Roman Catholic churches which sing mostly charismatic choruses, and United Reformed churches which use candles and liturgical colours. In the past, the worship in many denominations tended to be defined by what they didn't do! Anglicans didn't use extempore prayer, that was for the Free Churches; Methodists didn't use candles, that was for the Anglicans, and so on. It seems as if many of those barriers have now broken down. We may feel confused by this, or even threatened. After all, the style of worship has, in the past, been one of the things which most publicly helps to define what it means to be a particular kind of Christian.

This is now also often an issue within the local church itself. The housegroup tried to plan a service which would have something in it for everybody, but as Betty realized, there were limits to that. What they produced was a good example of a preaching service, characteristic of certain kinds of

Protestantism. This was because the members of the group all
came from that tradition, were more or less comfortable with it,
and worked with what they knew. Mollie, it would appear, is
mildly charismatic. She appreciates worship which enables her
to 'praise the Lord' as she puts it. She approved of the Anglican
service Christine and Alan went to, where people clapped and
raised their hands in the air. If there had been more members of
the group like Mollie, the service they planned might have had
more opportunity for praise songs, a time for testimonies to be
given and opportunity for members of the congregation to
minister to each other in prayer. That would almost certainly
not have helped Alan to worship. If there had been more people
in the group like him there probably wouldn't have been any
praise songs at the beginning, but there might have been five
hymns by Charles Wesley. These things can, and sometimes
do, cause real tensions within a worshipping community. How
has this variety come about?

FOR DISCUSSION: What changes have you noticed in the
worshipping life of your own congregation in the last five
years?

2. *The Reasons for Variety*

a. *The Liturgical Movement*
   Quite early in the process of planning the housegroup service,
Julie reacted badly to the word 'liturgy', assuming that it meant
the service would be read out of a book. In fact the word, which
comes from Greek, simply means 'the offering of service'. It
came, in time, to be applied to Christian worship, specifically
to Holy Communion. In our own context, therefore, a liturgy is
any order of service, and the texts which are part of it. Even an
entirely 'free' act of worship has a liturgical structure (if only
in the mind of the leader) and the songs and prayers are
themselves the liturgy, however informal.

What we sometimes call the 'Liturgical Movement' began in earnest in the early years of the twentieth century as a movement for renewal of worship within the Roman Catholic church. In particular, it aimed to increase congregational participation. Scholars from other churches became interested in what was happening, and ideas began to be shared across the denominations. By and large, this involved re-thinking the first principles of Christian worship in the light of what we know of its origins and history. In recent years this has led to the attempt to establish a common version of those texts which most Christians use, either regularly or occasionally; for example, the Lord's Prayer, the Gloria and the Te Deum. Liturgists do not work in a vacuum, and the results of their work can be seen not only in new service books in most major denominations, but in a continuing stream of new worship material, most of which is usable by Christians in all mainstream churches. The best-known examples of this come from Taizé and Iona.

b. *The Charismatic Movement*
This is usually reckoned to have begun in the United States in the 1960s. Experiences which had been previously thought of as belonging to the Pentecostal churches began to happen in other groups of Christians. Speaking and singing in tongues, resting in or being slain in the Spirit, visions and the laying on of hands for ministry or healing, are all characteristics of this movement. In some cases charismatic groups found their existing denominations unreceptive, and they broke away. The so-called House Churches often originated in this way. Many charismatic Christians, however, remained within their churches. Some parishes and congregations, in all mainstream denominations, have taken on a largely charismatic character. In those places there is room within the standard liturgy for charismatic expression. It is sometimes the case that those who have not shared the charismatic experience see only the

86

undoubted difficulties it can cause within a worshipping community, but this is unfortunate. Both the charismatic and liturgical movements have this in common: they are concerned that the worship should be truly the work of the congregation, not a performance by the preacher or priest. The charismatic experience has undoubtedly influenced most mainstream worship, not least through what we sing.

c. *The explosion of hymnody*

Hymns are one of the principal ways in which a congregation can participate directly in the worship. New hymns have been produced steadily since the seventeenth century, but in the twentieth century there has been what can only be described as an 'explosion' in the amount produced. New hymns are, of course, of all kinds. But the most noticeable change has been in the number which have come from the evangelical or charismatic wing of the church and quickly won acceptance in the mainstream denominations. This is perhaps the charismatic movement's most widespread contribution to the life of the whole church. Many of them are very simple, even by comparison with a traditional four-line common metre hymn. Some consist of little more than a verse of scripture, or a couple of short lines repeated several times. The music is often very easy to learn and in a more recognizably contemporary idiom than traditional hymnody. The widespread availability of such material, using modern technology, means that a huge variety of worship songs are now readily accessible to every congregation.

d. *Mobility*

The worshipping life of our churches is more affected by what have been called 'non-theological factors' than we sometimes realize. Undoubtedly one of the things which has helped to bring much greater variety within denominations and churches has been a more mobile population. People now move home more often and go on holiday to exotic places. Some, like Tom and Betty, experience worship when on holiday which is totally unlike anything they have met before. Some bring back ideas, practices or worship material to their home churches. When people move house, they may not automatically go to the local church of their former denomination. They may look around until they find a church which offers the kind of worship they find helpful, and then join it, regardless of which denomination it is part of. Of course, congregations have never been hermetically sealed units; but the arrival of new people with new ideas and experiences has never been as widespread as it is today. This is bound to affect the character of a congregation's worshipping life.

FOR DISCUSSION: Do you think any of the above (a-d) are significant factors in bringing about the changes you have already discussed?

3. *Is Variety a Problem?*

At first sight it looks as if it is! Christine wondered whether a hypothetical visitor from Mars would recognize all these different kinds of worship as Christian. Probably not, unless the visitor understood the language in which the worship was being held. Not understanding Greek made Betty and Tom's experience of worship somewhat puzzling. Julie, on the other hand, found that she could understand most of what was happening at a baptism in a Roman Catholic church. She even said that it 'wasn't really very different from the christenings we have at church' (the influence of the Liturgical Movement!). There are two major reasons why Christians worship in such different ways, and Betty summed them up as: 'Habit, and perhaps temperament'.

a. *Habit*

This is a rather unkind word. Perhaps 'tradition' would be better. We can think of the history of the Christian church as being rather like a family tree. There are many different branches of the Christian family, some of them quite close together, some of them rather more distant from others. Like natural families, each part of the Christian family has developed its own habits and customs.

When a couple are developing a relationship, perhaps moving towards engagement and marriage, one of the things they come to realize is that customs each of them has taken to be normal and standard may be no more than the practice of their own particular family: 'Oh, your father pays all the household bills, does he? Mum does that in our family,' or, 'Do you really wait until after Christmas dinner to open your presents? We stay up till midnight on Christmas Eve and open them then!' Some of the things which happen in worship may be no more than the custom of that particular part of the Christian family. A good example of a peculiarly Methodist family custom is that of taking Holy Communion 'in tables'.

More importantly, the worshipping tradition has developed differently in different denominations because of the needs of society at the time the church was formed, and the particular gifts of the people who have made up its life ever since. A denomination which was 'born in song' is likely to continue to make hymnody central to its worshipping life. A church which was founded on great preaching will inevitably develop and cherish a great preaching tradition. A religious society which sprang out of the conviction that we need to listen to the Spirit in every human being will treasure and value silence.

Of course, some parts of the Christian family may worship differently from others because of a deeply held belief. Some Christians, for example, find help in a service called Benediction, where there is adoration of, and blessing bestowed from, the reserved sacrament of consecrated bread. Other

89

Christians, as a matter of conviction, could not meaningfully share in such a service because they hold a different view of the presence of Christ at the Holy Communion. But such differences of belief actually affect what we do in worship less than we might suppose. Increasingly we are coming to realize this, and are finding in each other's traditions treasures which can enrich our own worship. The tensions which can arise are because, as we have already noted, the way in which we worshipped has often in the past been one of the major ways in which we have defined what kind of Christian we were. Increasingly this is no longer the case. Whether we find that fact confusing or exhilarating may largely depend on our temperament.

b. *Temperament*

One of the great fears aroused by ecumenism and moves towards church unity, even in the 1960s, was that it would mean 'uniformity'; that everyone would be expected to worship in the same way and that this would mean a denial of conscience and a suppression of individuality. Looking back, it seems incredible that this could ever have been such a worry to some of us. Since then, all the moves have been in the opposite direction! The most obvious example is the Church of England. Its worship was never as uniform as some imagined it to be, but at the end of the twentieth century it is arguably the least uniform denomination in Christendom so far as its worshipping life is concerned. Within its embrace can be found almost everything from Sung High Mass to 'alternative worship' with heavy metal music and not a book in sight! Indeed, the argument today is not whether we should all worship in the same way, but what, if any, are the acceptable limits of diversity.

It is a simple fact of human nature that we do not all find the same things helpful. We express ourselves in different ways. This, it might be argued, is as it should be. It does no more than reflect the glorious diversity of God's creation. The varying traditions of the church's worshipping life need not be seen as a problem. After all, response to what God has done in Jesus Christ lies at the heart of all of them.

FOR DISCUSSION: What problems has your worshipping congregation experienced as a result of changes which have taken place? How do you think these might be resolved?

4. *What is Worship all About?*

It is time to ask the question originally posed by Julie: why do we worship, and what does it achieve?

a. *Wonder and awe*

Most people have experienced a sense of wonder at some moment in their lives. For many people this comes about through such ordinary things as the sight of a majestic mountain range, or the first glimpse of a new-born baby. Others, especially in a scientific and technological age, find the intricacy and detail of a living organism or, say, the structure of DNA, an equal source of wonder. We may all wonder at the marvel of the human mind which can produce both computers that play chess, and the music of Mozart! What we discover at such times is that seemingly ordinary things are not so ordinary after all. We have a real sense of something which is beyond ourselves and our natural response is to want to say 'thank you'. This is a problem for atheists: to whom do they give thanks?

People of faith are not, as is sometimes supposed, simple-minded about such things. We know perfectly well that the majestic mountain range was produced by primaeval upheavals in the earth's crust, and that the music which moves us to tears was written by a human being. But there remains a sense of otherness, of something given to us. We receive it in gratitude, and give thanks to God who makes such marvels of beauty and truth possible. What we are doing, when we catch our breath at the sheer glory and wonder of things, is to *respond* to that which comes from beyond ourselves. As we do so, we find that the way we look at life begins to change. This is the fundamental impulse behind the offering of worship. But, of course, there are other things too.

b. *Gratitude and joy*

The General Thanksgiving from the *Book of Common Prayer* has a memorable phrase: 'We bless thee for our creation, preservation, and all the blessings of this life.' Over and above a sense of wonder at existence itself, is our sense of gratitude for the daily blessings we ourselves enjoy; the things which are specific to us. No sooner do we say this, than we are conscious that there are things in our lives, and in the lives of others, which are not blessings at all. We cannot bless God for the pain, sorrow and sin which marks so much of the human lot. Yet the very sense that life *ought* not to be full of pain somehow deepens our gratitude for the good things and at the same time makes us want to wrestle with God over the agonies. We call this prayer.

c. *What God has done*

The General Thanksgiving continues with the words, 'but above all, for thine inestimable love in the redemption of the world by our Lord Jesus Christ; for the means of grace, and for the hope of glory'. Here we move further into what lies behind *Christian* worship. In Christian worship the focus of our wonder and awe, gratitude and joy, is the story of what God has done in Jesus Christ.

The Prologue to John's Gospel expresses the heart of that story: 'And the word became flesh and lived among us, and we have seen his glory, the glory as of a father's only son, full of grace and truth' (John 1.14). Here is a daring claim indeed: that

God himself has taken human flesh and lived among us in the person of Jesus. It is the culmination of a long story, which we can read about in the Hebrew Scriptures (Old Testament). Christians believe that in the birth, life and teaching, and above all in the death and resurrection of Jesus, God is most fully revealed to us. Nor is that all. This is brought alive in every age, and in the life of every believer, through the continual activity of the Holy Spirit, given to the church at Pentecost. We respond to the story of Jesus, not just as an event of the past, but as something which has contemporary meaning and significance for us.

d. *Praise and adoration*

'I just wanted . . . to praise God for giving me such a wonderful Saviour in Jesus,' Mollie said. In a sense she was right, though she expressed it somewhat narrowly. At the heart of Christian worship is the desire to adore God, to make a response to what God has done in Christ. Yet it is easy to misunderstand this. C. S. Lewis wrote about the way in which, before he became a Christian, and even for some time afterwards, he found the requirement to 'praise God' a major stumbling block. We do not, after all, think much of a human being who constantly demands 'praise' from other people. Indeed, we suspect that such a person might even need psychiatric help! Why, then, is it considered so important to 'praise' God, and what picture of God does that give us? It was, C. S. Lewis wrote, some time before he realized what praise was really all about. He had been thinking about it as if it was like paying God a compliment. It isn't like that at all. On the contrary, the world is full of praise. Human beings naturally and spontaneously praise what they most care about and value. Indeed, praise does not merely express our joy and love. In some sense it adds to it. As C. S. Lewis expressed it: 'It is not out of compliment that lovers keep on telling one another how beautiful they are; the delight is incomplete until it is

93

expressed.' So when, for instance, the Psalmists urge us to praise God, that is not because God has an over-inflated ego and needs our praise. It is because *as* we praise and glorify God we enter into a fuller and deeper relationship with him.

e. *Listening*

If we are to praise and worship God because of what has been done for us in Christ then, of course, we must know what it is that has been done. Not just the story of Jesus, that may in itself be familiar enough. No, we need to hear the meaning and implications of that story as it bears upon our own lives and the world in which we live. So also central to worship is listening to God. The biblical story offers us the insights into what God's love means for us and the truth by which we may live. The Bible is a book of witnesses to God's involvement with the human race. So, in worship, we listen to the Bible being read and to the words of the preacher. We listen in worship, in order that we might respond, and be changed in the process.

f. *Engagement*

When we put together these two things, listening to God and responding to God, we can see that worship is essentially an engagement with God. We do not worship in order to know more about God, we worship in order to meet with God himself. Through worship, God offers himself in order that we may meet with him. In worship at its best, we are reconciled to God, empowered by God and become more fully what we already are – Christians.

But Julie's friend Fiona claimed that 'You don't need to go to church to be a Christian.' At one level it would seem that she is right. We can say our prayers, read our Bibles and even sing hymns of praise on our own. Why then is worship, in the Christian tradition, something which we do together?

There are many possible answers to that question. Some of them would take us well beyond the limits of a modest book on worship. Put simply: we were never meant to be Christians on our own. We need to take very seriously the New Testament picture of the church as 'the body of Christ' and of individual Christians as parts of it. We are, literally, incomplete as Christians without one another. By the same token, our 'private' worship is incomplete. It is as we share one another's joys, heal one another's hurts, encourage one another in the Christian life and bear one another's sorrows, that the full richness of our engagement with God begins to be seen.

God has called into being a community of faith which, whatever its obvious imperfections, is intended to be a sign of his love for the world. It is also intended to be a pointer to what the whole of human community should be like. We are not called to be Christians for the private blessings we receive, but in order that the world might be loved and served by the community which bears Christ's name. When we engage in our private devotions, we do so as members of the body of Christ, and we often make use of resources that fellow members of that body have provided for us. Then we gather together as a Christian congregation, united in the praise and worship of God. In doing so, we witness in a very public way to what we believe needs to be at the centre of human life – an engagement with God which changes things.

FOR DISCUSSION: What would need to happen in the life of your church to make Sunday worship more truly an engagement with God?

Further Reading

James F. White, *Introduction to Christian Worship*, Abingdon Press, Nashville 1980

Perhaps the best general introduction to the importance of liturgical studies for the contemporary Christian.

Susan J. White, *Groundwork of Christian Worship*, Epworth Press, 1997

Provides a structure for thinking seriously about worship as a part of Christian faith and experience, and points forward to learning about the church. A comprehensive introduction.

Alan Dunstan, *Interpreting Worship*, Mowbray 1984

Examines what our worship says about our understanding of God. Thought provoking and very accessible.

T. G. A. Baker, *Questioning Worship*, SCM Press 1977

A provocative little book, which posed sharp questions about what modern liturgists are saying, not all of which have been answered.

Ralph P. Martin, *The Worship of God*, Eerdmans, Grand Rapids 1983

A New Testament scholar takes a careful look at worship in today's church and at the theological rationale which underlies it.

David Peterson, *Engaging with God*, Apollos/IVP 1992

Explores what 'biblical worship' might be in a thorough, though highly individualistic, manner.

Further Reading

Graham Kendrick, *Worship*, Kingsway Publications 1984

With no pretensions to scholarship, the author writes clearly and helpfully about the purpose and practice of worship.

Laurence Hull Stookey, *Calendar: Christ's Time for the Church*, Abingdon Press, Nashville 1996

Gets to the heart of why there is a liturgical year.

John C. A. Barrett, *Family Worship*, Epworth Press 1982

A thoughtful exploration of most of the issues surrounding all-age worship.

Richard G. Jones, *Groundwork of Worship and Preaching*, Epworth Press 1980

For several years this was a textbook for those training to be Methodist Local Preachers. Now slightly dated, it is still a worthwhile introduction to the main issues.

David Buttrick, *A Captive Voice*, Westminster John Knox Press, Minneapolis 1994

Considers both the theory and method of preaching, largely from a preacher's perspective. More advanced reading.

Donald English, *An Evangelical Theology of Preaching*, Abingdon Press, Nashville 1996

An up to date study in how to communicate the gospel *for* today *to* today by a well-known Methodist leader.

Some of these books are out of print. Borrow them from your local library. Libraries can obtain books through inter-library loan.